Setting the Right Price
For Your
Design & Illustration

BARBARA GANIM

NORTH LIGHT BOOKS

Cincinnati, Ohio

Setting the Right Price For Your Design and Illustration. Copyright © 1994 by Barbara Ganim. Printed and bound in the United States of America. All rights reserved. No part of this book may be reproduced in any form or by any electronic or mechanical means including information storage and retrieval systems without permission in writing from the publisher, except by a reviewer, who may quote brief passages in a review. Published by North Light Books, an imprint of F&W Publications, Inc., 1507 Dana Avenue, Cincinnati, Ohio 45207. 1-800-289-0963. First edition.

98   97   96   95   94   5   4   3   2   1

Library of Congress Cataloging-in-Publication Data

Ganim, Barbara.
    Setting the right price for your design and illustration/Barbara Ganim.
        p.   cm.
    Includes index.
    ISBN 0-89134-569-8
    1. Commercial art—United States—Marketing. 2. Graphic arts—United States—
    Marketing.   I. Title.
NC1001.6.G36   1994
745.6'068'8—dc20   94-3840
                                                             CIP

Edited by Mary Cropper and Diana Martin
Interior and cover design by Brian Roeth

This book is dedicated to the one person who made it all possible: Mary Cropper,
my acquisition editor at North Light Books. She was more than an editor, she was in
many ways a supportive co-author.

A C K N O W L E D G M E N T S

To obtain the most up-to-date pricing and product information, I called on
other design and illustration professionals who were kind enough to share
their experiences and expert knowledge. I am not only grateful for their help,
but am still struck by their willingness to give me long stretches of valuable
time, often in the middle of a busy work day. I would like to thank these
people individually, and also apologize in advance if I unknowingly omit
anyone: Robert P. Bernier, architectural illustrator and member of the
American Society of Architectural Perspectivists; Don Childs, senior designer,
DiDonato Associates, Chicago, Illinois; Carol Buchanan, book jacket design-
er, C.A. Buchanan Designs, Matthews, North Carolina; Louise Fili, Louise Fili
Ltd., New York, New York; Michael Fleishman, freelance illustrator and
writer, Yellow Springs, Ohio; Randy Glasbergen, cartoonist *(The Better Half)*,
Sherburne, New York; Jean Miller Harding, medical illustrator, Ontario,
Canada; Linda Kondo, project manager, Clifford Selbert Design, Cambridge,
Massachusetts; Terri McDermott, certified medical illustrator, Elgin, Illinois;
Douglas Parker, art director, *Bostonia Magazine*, Boston, Massachusetts; Sarah
Speare, executive director, Society for Environmental Graphic Design,
Cambridge, Massachusetts.

I would also like to thank Diana Martin, my editor with North Light
Books, and Brian Roeth, designer at North Light for their gentle encourage-
ment, insight and manageable deadlines that kept this project on track. And
finally, my appreciation to my dear friend Liliana Costa for her creative con-
tributions to both the text and illustration aspects of this book, and her
patience and support as I grumbled and complained my way through some
of the more difficult parts of this project.

TABLE OF CONTENTS

S E C T I O N   F O U R
IT TAKES MORE THAN GOOD PRICES 143

A quick review of the basics of preparing a proposal, making presentations, putting together and showing a portfolio, effective negotiating, staying competitive and getting paid. Includes do's and don'ts and plenty of tips and tricks for success.

INTRODUCTION

When I look back on my early years of running a graphic design studio and advertising agency, I know the most difficult, and often agonizingly painful, part was pricing my work. It seemed almost impossible to learn everything I needed to know about how to price a project. Even worse, I didn't know what I needed to know to price a project. I had never worked for anyone, so I had no experience to draw on. I didn't even know another designer that I could ask for advice.

Once I did learn how to price, mostly by trial and error, it was still a headache. All I wanted to do was spend my time designing and illustrating, not punching numbers into a calculator and talking to printers about quotes. Sometimes an entire day would be lost as I tried to figure out a price estimate for a job I wasn't even sure I would get. And because I hated pricing, the process seemed to take forever.

It took years, but I finally learned how to breeze through price estimates by simplifying and streamlining how I did it. I found a method that worked for me and stuck to it. (Practice makes perfect in pricing, just as it does when you're learning to design.) Now, I've written this book to share what I've learned about pricing, because I know it will help you transform a painful process into a (virtually) painless one.

The first section of this book introduces all the terminology you need to know to prepare an estimate. You'll also find all the different pricing methods commonly used by designers and illustrators, as well as the clients who hire them. Plus, you will get some tips on what's good to do and what's good to avoid, if you possibly can, when you are faced with the many alternative pricing practices that are used in this industry.

In sections two and three, you can leave the theory behind and work through calculating what your hourly rate should be and what to charge for different projects. Rather than dull pages of formulas and figures, the worksheets are in a gameboard format. Each stage of calculating your rate or project cost is broken down into small, manageable chunks to simplify the process.

When you follow a worksheet with its sample project from the start to the goal, you will see what factors you need to consider when pricing each part of a job. There's plenty of room next to the sample in each box for you to

work out your price for a project. You'll also learn how to anticipate problems that could affect project pricing and see how to build in a margin for extra costs and other hidden surprises that can cost you money. You may want to photocopy the worksheets and write on those, so you can easily use a worksheet for more than one project.

The last section of the book deals with other areas of having a design studio that affect and are affected by pricing. Here, you'll find the information you need to put together a proposal, make a presentation, negotiate with clients and vendors, stay competitive and get paid.

To get the most from this book, I recommend that you read the first section of the book before exploring the worksheets. I've kept it short and to the point, since I know you have things you'd rather be doing. Skim quickly through the glossary at the end of that section; you can refer back to it if you need to remember what a term means when you're doing a worksheet.

If you haven't already determined an hourly rate for your design and illustration work, choose the worksheet in section two that best applies to your business situation. Follow the example provided, then fill in the spaces in the box with information about your own expenses.

Flip through the third section to see which worksheets deal with the kinds of projects you are presently working on, or those you could get in the future. The examples will show you how to price projects you've never had before. When you need to price a certain kind of project, use a blank worksheet (better yet, photocopy the worksheet so you can reuse it) and follow the example to work out your own prices.

Once you've started to improve your pricing skills, you may want to work on your presentation strategy or learn new techniques for successful negotiation with clients and vendors. You'll find ideas for all this and more in section four.

Concepts, Principles and Practices

Pricing is the tool you use to determine what to charge clients for your creativity and your time and what the services and materials you purchase for them cost. Most designers really hate and fear pricing (I do, too), but getting the right price for your work is the best way to ensure that you can do what you love—design or illustration.

Because I didn't like pricing, I would put it off until the last minute or labor over it for hours in pursuit of the "right" price. Finally, I realized that it would be better to pick one method of pricing and always do it the same way, so I could do it faster and better (and get it over with). It took time and effort to master this skill because I didn't have anyone to help me figure it out. I hope this book will save you that time and trouble.

In this chapter you'll learn the basics of the method I teach in this book. This will give you an overview of the whole process before you have to get involved with all the details. Although this method has worked for me for many years, I will review some of the other ways designers price their work—and the advantages and disadvantages of each. You'll also find tips for what to do and what to avoid when pricing your work.

The last part of the chapter is a glossary of terms, principles and practices commonly used in pricing. Each term is defined and then explained in the context of how you would use it when pricing a design or illustration project. You may find it helpful to skim through these terms now, reading those that aren't familiar to you. You can then refer back to this section to refresh your memory about specific terms as you use the worksheets in the rest of the book.

Pricing is a skill that you, as a designer or illustrator, must master if you want to survive and thrive in your business. You may argue that talent and love of your craft are enough. But, for most people that just isn't so. Failure to properly price a project has sent many freelancers and entrepreneurs back to staff jobs, tails between their legs. This book's step-by-step format gives creatives the pricing how-to needed to succeed independently as artists.

WHAT IS PRICING?

Simply put, pricing is what you need to charge a client in order to stay in business. More specifically, it is what you charge to design or to illustrate the client's ad, brochure, identity systems, etc. And, most importantly, pricing must pay for your creativity, time and expenses; outside services you arrange; usage rights to the work; and a profit.

Pricing is inherently a complex process. Yet, just as you learned to design step by step, you can learn, step by step, how to price your work. The important considerations, factors and methods are covered throughout this book and its comprehensive, interactive worksheets.

FEAR OF PRICING

For many artists, the fear of pricing a job is often worse than the reality. But by breaking the task down into manageable steps, it can be a quick process. And, the more you do it, the easier it becomes. Past job records (of hours, expenses, suppliers, costs, etc.) are helpful tools for pricing new jobs.

Pricing should not be thought of as a marketing strategy in which prices are lowballed or kept very low in order to attract clients. The only long-term result from this is an unstable client base. Rather than hiring you for your excellent service, result-oriented work and quality product, they hire you for your low prices and leave when a new kid makes a better offer.

Another fallacy newcomers believe is that even if they cut their prices to hook clients, they can make up their loss in volume. This only works for discount stores. It won't work for you because you still have to spend the hours to do a job, there are only so many hours in a day, and you can crank out only so many jobs.

PRICING YOUR WORK

There are many ways to price your work, and you will find that the project's circumstances often dictate which one is used.

The most common method is hourly rate. Your cost for doing a project is figured based upon a per hour fee (which covers the cost of doing business, plus some profit) times the number of hours the project is expected to take. The variable hourly rate method is used most often by designers and is simply charging different hourly rates for different types of work, such as creative versus paste-up. In section two are six worksheets/gameboards that will help you quickly figure out your own hourly rate, based on your situation.

Once you set your hourly rate(s), you should consider project usage when pricing a job. Project usage (or Rights of Reproduction) is how a client is going to print and distribute your work. Common usage is typically "one time," that is, the work is printed and distributed only once within a project's guidelines (e.g., a brochure, magazine cover or ad).

When a client wants to exceed one-time usage, each subsequent usage (e.g., use of a magazine cover in a direct mail campaign) requires an additional charge. The concept of usage is more complex than can be explained here, since issues include not just the concrete form in which your work appears but also the scope of its distribution (local, national or international). Consult the Graphic Artists Guild's *Handbook of Pricing & Ethical Guidelines* for in-depth information.

Hourly rate and usage pricing are the fairest methods because you are paid for your time and the use of the finished piece. It is critical that as you use the pricing worksheets in this book you don't underestimate your time and that you always get a client to spell out (prior to quoting a final price) how he wants to use your work.

Many artists use alternative methods of pricing their work. Page-rate pricing is used by designers who do the same type of project regularly, such as annual reports or brochures. Familiarity with the needs of certain formats results in fairly reliable page rates. Before finalizing a quote, be sure that a project's specifications are consistent with your experience on these projects and that you are up-to-date on the costs of outside services, especially if you must oversee and bill for these services.

Magazine and newspaper design or illustration (cover, editorial or advertising) is sometimes priced from a page rate based on the publication's advertising page rate, which reflects circulation and geographical distribution. Since these page rates are usually not negotiable, make sure the client's budget covers your hours and expenses.

Budgeted pricing occurs when a client has a specific dollar amount, sometimes a range, attached to a project. Sometimes the budget is negotiable. Again, carefully calculate your time, expenses and usage to see if you can afford to do the project and make a profit.

Going-rate, or market-rate, pricing is the practice of pricing based on what others in your geographical market charge. This could apply to your hourly or page rate. Going rate is a useful barometer of whether or not your pricing is competitive, but it isn't a sound pricing method since it encourages lowballing and undermines your creative worth (not to mention your income).

Past project pricing, which is quoting the same price you charged for a similar piece last year (or even last month), is also unsound. Costs for outside services (printing, type, etc.) are always on the rise, and your quotes must keep pace. And, no

---

TWELVE WAYS TO AVOID LOSING MONEY ON A PROJECT

It is easy to make sure you don't lose money on a project by following specific business policies.

1. Shop around for outside services (type, printing, etc.), get at least two bids, and get them in writing.
2. Don't underestimate the number of hours a project will take.
3. On projects with ultratight deadlines, negotiate for more time or charge overtime (time-and-a-half or a percentage of the total project cost).
4. Put in writing the number of revision rounds the project includes and notify the client of the cost of excessive rounds.
5. If the client makes changes that affect your quote, immediately inform the client in writing of the added costs.
6. Always use a work order or client contract and be sure it states your payment policies.
7. Check in your business community about a new client's reputation regarding payment, reliability and ethics.
8. Do your math right. Double check your figures.
9. Get suppliers to fix their quotes for a specific time period. Make them requote after that.
10. Refigure your hourly rate twice a year or as your operating expenses increase to be sure you are covering your costs in your fees.
11. Make sure when you work for a flat fee that it covers your expenses and time.
12. Bill clients as soon as projects are done.

---

matter how similar projects seem, each has its peculiarities, which affects your cost.

In the book publishing, greeting card and cartoon industries is a standard type of payment. A royalty is a (sometimes negotiable) percentage of a product's price, usually its wholesale or net price. If you work on a royalty basis, you may get a monetary advance to cover your time and expenses. The advance varies, and your client will "pay himself back" by deducting the advance from your royalties. If the product doesn't sell as well as expected, you do not repay the advance. Make sure that your contract stipulates this arrangement. It is wise to consult a contract lawyer before signing a royalty-based contract.

Designers, more commonly than

illustrators, are starting to ask clients to commit to a six-month or one-year service contract, with a specific sum of money paid on a monthly basis as a service binder. Subsequent design and consultation services are billed against the retainer. The advantages of this method are the guarantee of multiple projects, a long-term designer-client relationship and regular cash flow. The disadvantages are that clients will call too often about minor issues and will expect priority over nonretainer-paying clients. Also, some clients may begin to question whether they are getting back in service what they pay out.

Before you start working on a retainer basis, elicit advice from other designers engaged in this pricing method. Discuss the issue with your lawyer and accountant as well, since they may also use this method of billing clients.

A final aspect of pricing involves billing the costs of outside services such as type, printing, service bureau output, and so forth. You can order and pay for all outside services and then be reimbursed for these costs by the client as part of your final bill. In this case add a markup, generally 15 to 20 percent, to the costs of those services. That markup pays for your time in obtaining those services and com-pensates you for paying out money before the client pays you.

Many designers prefer an arrangement where they serve as print buyers and supervisors, but the client is billed directly by the printer, service bureau, photographer and other vendors. In these cases designers retain responsibility for and authority over quality control, but they don't risk getting stuck with a large printing bill if a client can't or won't pay. When the designer is the print broker, she generally receives a fee from the printer. When the designer has contractual oversight, he charges the client for his time spent checking proofs and working with the printer.

As a designer, you can frequently negotiate a better price for services, especially printing, than a client can. You can also maintain better quality control and manage the production schedule if you directly supervise all production activities. These are arguments to give a client who insists on making all the arrangements for production services when they're billed directly.

PRICING TERMS, PRINCIPLES AND PRACTICES

The definitions in this glossary explain the terms, principles and practices that are common in your business and that are used through-out this book and its worksheets/ gameboards.

Advance: A portion of the total cost of a project paid before the project begins or all work is finished. In general request at least one-third of the total cost before work begins, another third part way through the job, and the last third on completion. This ensures that you'll get at least partial payment if the client can't or won't pay promptly—or at all—when the job is done. In tough economic times, ask for half of your money up front for additional security.

Benefits: As a self-employed person, you should provide yourself with benefits, such as health and disability insurance, a paid vacation, and a leased or purchased business vehicle.

Billable expenses: These are project-related expenses passed along to the client, including mileage, supplies, phone calls, faxes, postage, research, service bureau charges and typesetting.

Billable hours: This includes planning and creative time billed to the client. *See* nonbillable hours.

Budget: The money a client sets aside for a project. It is your responsibility to stay within the budget once you give a quote, even if your actual costs run higher. The client is responsible for costs resulting from midproject changes.

Cancellation/kill fee: This is an agreed-to fee that you get if a client cancels a project once the work begins or if the client rejects your completed work and fires you. A cancellation fee is often included in the contract.

Client requirements: These are elements a client desires or requires of the project, such as the quality of the final product and the kind of service expected. Always consider how a client's requirements might increase a project's complexity and your costs.

Complexity of job: Project pricing depends upon how complex it is; i.e., what is involved in producing the job. To assess complexity, consider things such as the project's specs (size, number of colors and visuals) and the outside services needed (writer, artists, etc.).

Consultation: In a consultation, a designer evaluates a client's graphic design needs and recommends solutions and procedures. Creative and production services are usually not required.

Copyright: The U.S. Copyright Law of 1978 gives you control over how, when and where your work is used by a client. You may transfer this ownership to a client, usually for a fee.

Estimate: Also called a price

quote, this is the approximate cost of completing a project based on your time, expenses, and the client's use of the piece.

Flat fee: Usually not negotiable, this is a set fee a client is willing to pay for a specific project.

Going rate: This is an hourly or per project form of pricing based on what others in your geographical market charge.

Hidden surprise factor: A project estimate should include a percentage of your total cost to cover unexpected problems and costs. Add 5 percent for direct, fairly easy projects, up to 25 percent as the project's complexity increases.

Hourly fee rate: This is the amount of money you charge per hour for your services.

Licensing: This lets someone manufacture your work as a marketable product (e.g., gift item, greeting card or calendar) for a specific time period, after which the licensed rights revert to you. You keep the copyright and receive an advance and royalties.

Lowballing: Some graphic artists who find out what other artists are quoting on a project will submit a lower quote in order to receive the job. Lowballing is considered unethical and devalues your creative work.

Markup: You can increase profits by charging a markup on materials and outside services, such as type, stats, film and printing. Standard markup most designers charge is 15 to 20 percent of the total cost for project expenses, although you can charge up to 100 percent for projects that require a twenty-four-hour turnaround. Experienced creatives charge a higher markup than beginners. A valuable project with a low budget may be worth lowering your markup for.

Nonbillable hours: Time spent on activities unrelated to the planning or creative needs of a project cannot be billed to a client. These include office management, general correspondence, bill paying, filing, record keeping and training (even if it is project-related).

Overhead: The total cost of operating a business is the overhead. Expenses include rent, utilities, insurance, salaries, benefits, self-promotion (brochures, business cards, stationery), furnishings, etc.

Overtime: This is time beyond the eight-hour day or forty-hour work week that is spent completing a project due to a tight, client-imposed deadline. Inform a client of expected overtime and related charges when you quote a job. Charges can be time-and-a-half (your hourly fee plus 50 percent times the number of O.T. hours),

double time (twice your hourly fee times O.T. hours) or a percentage (e.g., 5 percent). Set your own O.T. rate and use it consistently.

Page rate for designers: When a designer does the same type of project regularly (e.g., brochures or annual reports), it is often easier to set a standard page rate to use when quoting a project.

Page rate pricing for publications: The design or illustration of a magazine cover, an editorial page or an ad usually pays a page rate based on a percentage of the publication's ad page rate.

Pro bono work: This is unpaid work done for a worthy cause. Many artists annually spend a certain percentage of their time doing pro bono projects that serve as tax deductions and often offer much creative freedom. Consult your accountant before engaging in such work.

Profit: Also called net income, this is the money remaining when you subtract overhead expenses from income.

Revisions: These are client- or artist-recommended changes done at any stage of a design or an illustration. The extent of allowable revisions is negotiated with the client, within the budgetary framework; two rounds of revisions are standard. Extra rounds will normal-

ly incur added costs.

Rush charge: When vendors are asked to provide materials or services within an unreasonable amount of time (often less than twenty-four hours' notice), a rush charge is usually added to the cost. Ask if rush charges will be applied and how much they are. You should then pass that information on to the client, since that additional cost will be reflected in the final bill, changing the original quote.

When you are given a rush project, add your usual overtime charge or percentage for rush work. Many designers charge time-and-a-half for overtime; some charge double time for holidays and Sundays. Adding a percentage to the total time costs to cover rush charges is also common; for example, if the total project time cost was $1,200 and your rush charge percentage was 20 percent, a rush charge on that job would be $240 ($1,200 x .2 (20%)).

Sales tax: If your state has a sales tax—and most do—then 90 percent of the work you do as a graphic designer is taxable. State divisions of taxation put out booklets that clearly spell out what is and isn't taxable; they will also tell you how to get your permit to make sales at retail. Get the information from the taxation people or work with a knowledgeable accountant. You can't afford to make a mistake about taxes.

Speculative (spec) work: Work done on spec allows a client to decide if he wants to pay for a project after you complete it. This practice is considered unfair and unethical and is strongly discouraged industrywide.

Usage: Designers and illustrators price their work, in part, according to its end use. The broader a client's usage, the more rights he must pay for, and the higher the usage fee he is charged. Common usage, or rights of reproduction, are given below:

Exclusive Rights to a piece of art means that only the client can use it. An All Rights buy out means the client owns the work. In each case, the price reflects those rights purchased. Always have the client spell out exactly what is meant.

A Nonexclusive Rights agreement means that the client uses the work for a specified purpose during a limited period of time. The creator agrees not to sell those usage rights to someone else during that time period. When the time period is up, the creator can sell the use of the work to another client, if desired.

Variable rates: Some designers vary their fees for different services. Creative services are billed at the highest hourly rate. Client meetings may also be charged at the highest rate due to the people skills involved. Paste-up and clerical work are often priced about one-third less.

Work for hire: A work-for-hire agreement with a client transfers authorship and ownership of your work to the client and excludes you from any compensation for loss of the copyright and its future earnings. This practice is discouraged industrywide.

Setting Your Hourly Rate

These worksheets walk you through all the factors you need to consider when setting a basic Hourly Rate for your design or illustration. To make it easier, and a lot more fun, to determine the rate you'll charge for each hour of your design time, each worksheet is set up as a gameboard with a box for each expense involved in running your own studio or being a free-lancer.

Find the worksheet that most closely matches your current situation—or the one you'd like to grow into—and follow the example on the left-hand side of each box around the gameboard to set your own rate. The example in each box lists many of the factors or items that you need to consider when determining your monthly operating expenses. Skip boxes that don't apply to your situation, but otherwise fill in the boxes until you reach the Goal. For example, one box covers the cost of equipment leases; if you've bought all your equipment outright and don't plan to lease, you won't need to fill in an amount here.

Keep in mind that the ballpark figures given as examples here are only generic costs and salaries; they are not intended to represent what you definitely will earn or must expect to pay out. Use your actual costs for items such as rent, utilities and equipment whenever possible. If you don't have actual numbers, estimate these costs based on your friends' experiences, information from the utility company and other sources.

The Hourly Rate that you find when you follow the gameboard boxes from Start to Goal is an average or base rate that lets you cover your expenses and make a profit. Many designers are surprised when they compare what they ought to be charging to what they are charging. Often that indicates they've simply been charging too little. But what you are able to charge per hour also depends on the market for design in your area and the state of the economy. Sometimes a depressed economy or an oversized pool of design talent can push prices down. If that is the case in your area, concentrate on cutting your expenses or factor in a lower percentage for profit.

If you want to use variable rate pricing, your highest and your lowest rates should average out to at least the Hourly Rate. For example, your Hourly Rate works out at $40/hour, but you don't think you can charge that much for production work. You could charge $25/hour for production work and balance that with a charge of $55/hour for client meetings and concept development.

WORKSHEET 1

YOU ARE A FREELANCER WORKING AT HOME

This worksheet covers all possible expenses for a full-time designer with a fully outfitted home studio, but you can use this form even if you're only working part time and have very little income or equipment.

To know what hourly fees you need to charge to pay your bills and make a little money, too, fill in the dollar amounts requested as you move through the gameboard. Skip boxes that do not apply to you, but otherwise fill in the boxes in order until you reach the goal. The space on the left side of each box in the worksheet has been filled in to show you how a sheet for someone like you would look.

START

1 YOUR IN-HOME OFFICE RENT

EXAMPLE
$150/mo
- (When working at home, charge yourself at least minimal rent—a percentage of the rent or mortgage.)

YOUR COST
$_____/mo
-

2 YOUR SALARY

EXAMPLE
$2,000/mo
- (This is money to live on for a full-time freelance designer, but allow yourself a salary even if you're only freelancing part time. How much of a salary you can afford and whether it increases over time will help you tell when you're ready to be your own boss full time.)

YOUR COST
$_____/mo
-

5 INSURANCE

EXAMPLE
$250/mo
- Health
- Equipment/business
- Premises

YOUR COST
$_____/mo
-
-
-

4 TAXES

EXAMPLE
$400/mo
- Quarterly estimated self-employment tax
- Sales taxes

YOUR COST
$_____/mo
-
-

3 UTILITIES

EXAMPLE
$40/mo
- Electric
- Heat
- Air conditioning
- Phone
- Water/sewage

YOUR COST
$_____/mo
-
-
-
-
-

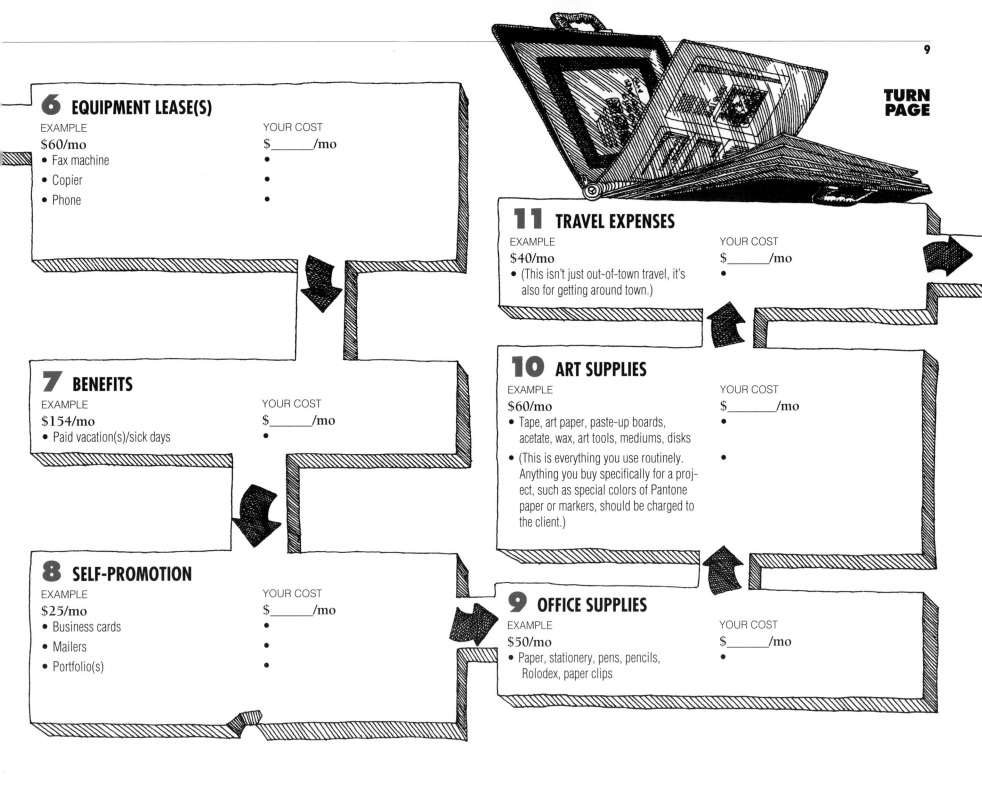

TURN PAGE

6 EQUIPMENT LEASE(S)

EXAMPLE
$60/mo
- Fax machine
- Copier
- Phone

YOUR COST
$_____/mo
-
-
-

11 TRAVEL EXPENSES

EXAMPLE
$40/mo
- (This isn't just out-of-town travel, it's also for getting around town.)

YOUR COST
$_____/mo
-

7 BENEFITS

EXAMPLE
$154/mo
- Paid vacation(s)/sick days

YOUR COST
$_____/mo
-

10 ART SUPPLIES

EXAMPLE
$60/mo
- Tape, art paper, paste-up boards, acetate, wax, art tools, mediums, disks
- (This is everything you use routinely. Anything you buy specifically for a project, such as special colors of Pantone paper or markers, should be charged to the client.)

YOUR COST
$_____/mo
-
-

8 SELF-PROMOTION

EXAMPLE
$25/mo
- Business cards
- Mailers
- Portfolio(s)

YOUR COST
$_____/mo
-
-
-

9 OFFICE SUPPLIES

EXAMPLE
$50/mo
- Paper, stationery, pens, pencils, Rolodex, paper clips

YOUR COST
$_____/mo
-

WORKSHEET 1 *CONTINUED*

16 SAVINGS FOR RETIREMENT: ADD $166.67/MO TO AMOUNT IN BOX 15

EXAMPLE
$3,835.67/mo
($3,669.00 + 166.67)
• (If you want to make a yearly contribution to an IRA, KEOGH or other retirement fund, $166.67/mo falls safely within the maximum you can put aside.)

YOUR COST
$_____/mo
•

12 BUSINESS ENTERTAINMENT

EXAMPLE
$40/mo

YOUR COST
$_____/mo

13 EQUIPMENT PURCHASES

EXAMPLE
$300/mo
• (This is usually part of your start-up costs but stays roughly the same amount after the first year. Budget at least a small amount for replacement if you have no ongoing expenses. I figured this on an initial outlay of $3,600, broken down into monthly payments.)

• Computer
• Printer
• Waxer
• Light box

YOUR COST
$_____/mo
•

•
•
•
•

15 TOTAL BOXES 1–14 TO GET YOUR BASIC MONTHLY OPERATING COSTS

EXAMPLE
$3,669/mo

YOUR COST
$_____/mo

14 FURNITURE PURCHASES

EXAMPLE
$100/mo
• (This is figured on the same basis as equipment—an initial outlay of $1,200, broken down into monthly payments.)

• Desk
• Chair(s)
• Drawing board
• Table(s)
• Computer stand
• Printer stand
• Bulletin board

YOUR COST
$_____/mo
•

•
•
•
•
•
•
•

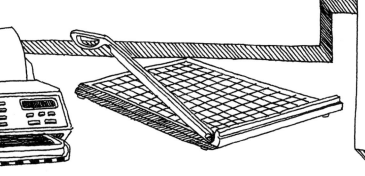

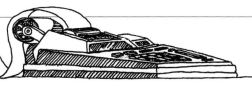

17 MULTIPLY THE TOTAL IN BOX 16 BY 10-20%, IF YOU WANT TO MAKE A PROFIT

EXAMPLE
$575.35/mo
($3,835.67 x .15(15%))

YOUR COST
$_____/mo

- (If you want to make any profit beyond your salary and retirement fund contribution, you have to figure that into your rate. It's not really an expense, but it's best to include it here.)

•

18 ADD BOXES 16 AND 17 TO GET YOUR TOTAL MONTHLY OPERATING COSTS

EXAMPLE
$4,411.02/mo

YOUR COST
$_____/mo

19 DIVIDE THE TOTAL IN BOX 18 BY 4 TO GET YOUR WEEKLY OPERATING COSTS

EXAMPLE
$1,102.76/wk
($4,411.02 / 4)

YOUR COST
$_____/wk

- (That's 4 for 4 weeks/month.)
  (4 weeks per month is used because 48 working weeks per year is what you'll realistically work. That allows 4 weeks of vacation, sick days and holidays—the yearly average taken by most self-employed designers.)

•

21 DIVIDE THE AMOUNT IN BOX 20 BY 6 TO GET YOUR HOURLY RATE: $36.76/HR

GOAL

EXAMPLE
- Round that amount up or down to the nearest even dollar to get your Hourly Rate...$37/hr
  (That's 6 for 6 billable hours in the average work day. Although you may be in your studio every day for at least eight hours, you'll probably never come up with more than six hours per day that you can actually bill to a client.)

- If you're only working part time, you may still want to assume you have a 5-day, 6-billable-hours-per-day week. That will be much easier than trying to estimate the number of days and hours you actually will work. You'll make less money that way, but if you have another source of income—your regular job, in other words—you can afford to make less when you're starting.

- If you want to see the results of working fewer days or hours per week, simply plug those numbers into Boxes 19 and 20.

YOUR COST
$_____/hr

•

•

20 DIVIDE THE AMOUNT IN BOX 19 BY 5 TO GET YOUR DAILY OPERATING COSTS

EXAMPLE
$220.55/day
($1,102.76 / 5)
- (That's 5 for 5 work days in a week.)

YOUR COST
$_____/day

•

WORKSHEET 2

YOU ARE A FREELANCER/SOLO DESIGNER WITH A STUDIO

This worksheet covers all possible expenses for a full-time designer with a studio away from home. Use this sheet whether you're starting out or have had your studio for a while. To know what hourly fees you need to charge to pay your bills and make a little money, too, fill in the dollar amounts requested as you move through the gameboard. Skip boxes that do not apply to you, but otherwise fill in the boxes in order until you reach the Goal. The space on the left side of each box in the worksheet has been filled in to show you how a sheet for someone like you would look.

START

1 YOUR STUDIO RENT

EXAMPLE
$400/mo

YOUR COST
$_____/mo

2 YOUR SALARY

EXAMPLE
$2,250/mo
• Money to live on

YOUR COST
$_____/mo
•

5 INSURANCE

EXAMPLE
$400/mo
• Health
• Equipment/business
• Premises

YOUR COST
$_____/mo
•
•
•

4 TAXES

EXAMPLE
$800/mo
• Quarterly estimated self-employment tax
• Sales taxes

YOUR COST
$_____/mo
•
•

3 UTILITIES

EXAMPLE
$120/mo
• Electric
• Heat
• Air conditioning
• Phone

YOUR COST
$_____/mo
•
•
•
•

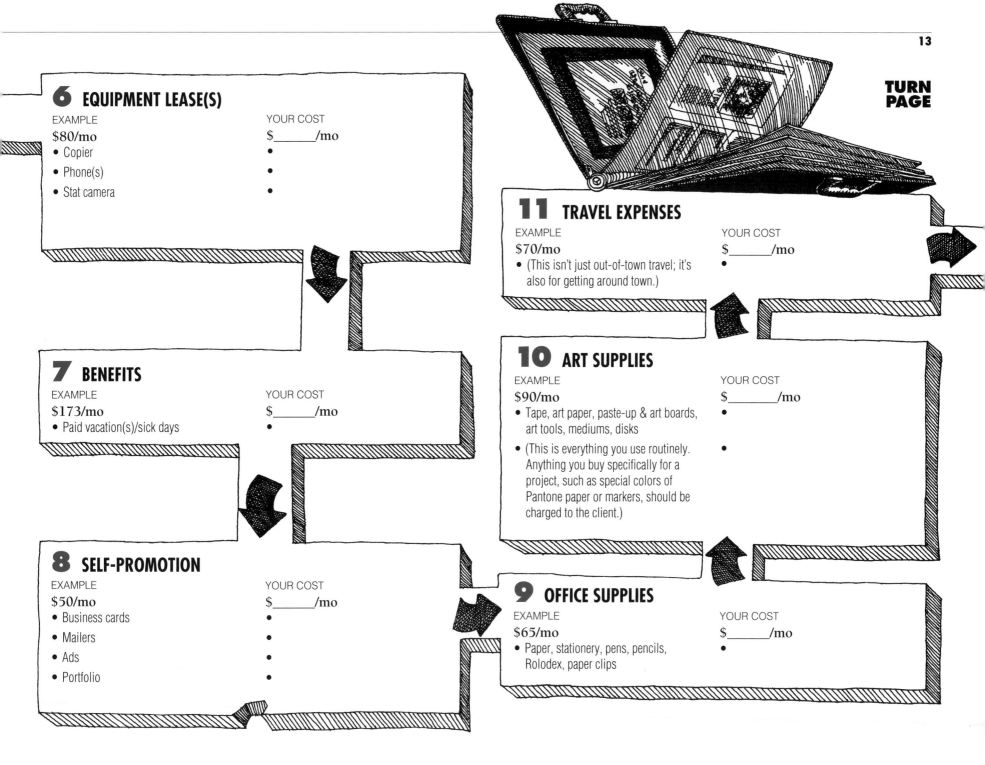

TURN PAGE

6 EQUIPMENT LEASE(S)

EXAMPLE
$80/mo
- Copier
- Phone(s)
- Stat camera

YOUR COST
$_____/mo
-
-
-

7 BENEFITS

EXAMPLE
$173/mo
- Paid vacation(s)/sick days

YOUR COST
$_____/mo
-

8 SELF-PROMOTION

EXAMPLE
$50/mo
- Business cards
- Mailers
- Ads
- Portfolio

YOUR COST
$_____/mo
-
-
-
-

11 TRAVEL EXPENSES

EXAMPLE
$70/mo
- (This isn't just out-of-town travel; it's also for getting around town.)

YOUR COST
$_____/mo
-

10 ART SUPPLIES

EXAMPLE
$90/mo
- Tape, art paper, paste-up & art boards, art tools, mediums, disks
- (This is everything you use routinely. Anything you buy specifically for a project, such as special colors of Pantone paper or markers, should be charged to the client.)

YOUR COST
$_____/mo
-
-

9 OFFICE SUPPLIES

EXAMPLE
$65/mo
- Paper, stationery, pens, pencils, Rolodex, paper clips

YOUR COST
$_____/mo
-

WORKSHEET 2 *CONTINUED*

16 SAVINGS FOR RETIREMENT: ADD $166.67/MO TO AMOUNT IN BOX 15

EXAMPLE
$5,204.67/mo
($5,038.00 + 166.67)

• (If you want to make a yearly contribution to an IRA or other type of retirement fund, $166.67/mo falls safely within the maximum you can put aside.)

YOUR COST
$_____/mo

•

12 BUSINESS ENTERTAINMENT

EXAMPLE
$40/mo

YOUR COST
$_____/mo

13 EQUIPMENT PURCHASES

EXAMPLE
$300/mo

• (This is usually a part of initial start-up costs and stays roughly the same amount after the first year. Budget at least a small amount for replacement if you have no ongoing expenses. I figured this on an initial outlay of $3,600, broken down into monthly payments.)

• Computer
• Fax machine
• Printer
• Waxer
• Light box

YOUR COST
$_____/mo

•

•
•
•
•
•

15 TOTAL BOXES 1–14 TO GET YOUR BASIC MONTHLY OPERATING COSTS

EXAMPLE
$5,038/mo

YOUR COST
$_____/mo

14 FURNITURE PURCHASES

EXAMPLE
$200/mo

• (This is figured on the same basis as equipment—an initial outlay of $2,400, broken down into monthly payments.)

• Desk
• Chair(s)
• Drawing Board
• Table(s)
• Printer stand
• Computer stand
• Bulletin board

YOUR COST
$_____/mo

•

•
•
•
•
•
•
•

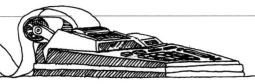

17 MULTIPLY THE TOTAL IN BOX 16 BY 10-20%, IF YOU WANT TO MAKE A PROFIT

EXAMPLE
$780.70/mo
($5,204.67 x .15(15%))

- (If you want to make any profit beyond your salary and retirement fund contribution, you have to figure that into your rate. It's not really an expense, but it's best to include it here.)

YOUR COST
$_____/mo

-

18 ADD BOXES 16 AND 17 TO GET YOUR TOTAL MONTHLY OPERATING COSTS

EXAMPLE
$5,985.37/mo

YOUR COST
$_____/mo

19 DIVIDE THE TOTAL IN BOX 18 BY 4 TO GET YOUR WEEKLY OPERATING COSTS

EXAMPLE
$1,496.34/wk
($5,985.37 / 4)

- (That's 4 for 4 weeks/month.)
- (4 weeks per month is used because 48 working weeks per year is what you'll realistically average. That allows 4 weeks of vacation, sick days and holidays—the yearly average taken by most self-employed designers.)

YOUR COST
$_____/wk

-
-

21 DIVIDE THE AMOUNT IN BOX 20 BY 6 TO GET YOUR HOURLY RATE: $49.88/HR

EXAMPLE

- Round that amount up or down to the even dollar to get your Hourly Rate $50/hr
- (That's 6 for 6 billable hours in the average work day. Although you may be in your studio every day for at least 8 hours, you'll probably never come up with more than 6 hours per day that you can actually bill to a client.)
- If you want to see the results of working fewer days or hours per week, simply plug those numbers into Boxes 19 and 20.

YOUR COST
$_____/hr

-

-

20 DIVIDE THE AMOUNT IN BOX 19 BY 5 TO GET YOUR DAILY OPERATING COSTS

EXAMPLE
$299.27/day
($1,496.34 / 5)

- (That's 5 for 5 work days in a week.)

YOUR COST
$_____/day

-

GOAL

WORKSHEET 3

YOU AND ANOTHER DESIGNER ARE PARTNERS

This worksheet covers 2 people sharing a studio and expenses 50-50. Use this worksheet for a partner or an association (two independent business entities with shared income and expenses). To know what hourly fees you need to charge to pay bills and make money, too, fill in the dollar amounts requested as you move through the gameboard. Skip boxes that do not apply to you, but otherwise fill in the boxes in order until you reach the Goal. The space on the left side of each box in the worksheet has been filled in to show you how a sheet for someone like you would look.

1 YOUR IN-HOME OFFICE RENT

EXAMPLE
$700/mo
- (When working at home, charge yourself at least minimal rent—a percentage of the rent or mortgage.)

YOUR COST
$_____/mo
-

2 YOUR SALARY

EXAMPLE
$6,000/mo
- (This is money to live on. Each partner is drawing a salary of $3,000/mo from their combined income. In an association, either person may also take solo projects and, therefore, have a different income or salary from the other.)

YOUR COST
$_____/mo
-

5 INSURANCE

EXAMPLE
$800/mo
- Health
- Equipment/business
- Premises

YOUR COST
$_____/mo
-
-
-

4 TAXES

EXAMPLE
$2,000/mo
- Quarterly estimated taxes
- Sales taxes

YOUR COST
$_____/mo
-
-

3 UTILITIES

EXAMPLE
$240/mo
- Electric
- Heat
- Air conditioning
- Phone

YOUR COST
$_____/mo
-
-
-
-

TURN PAGE

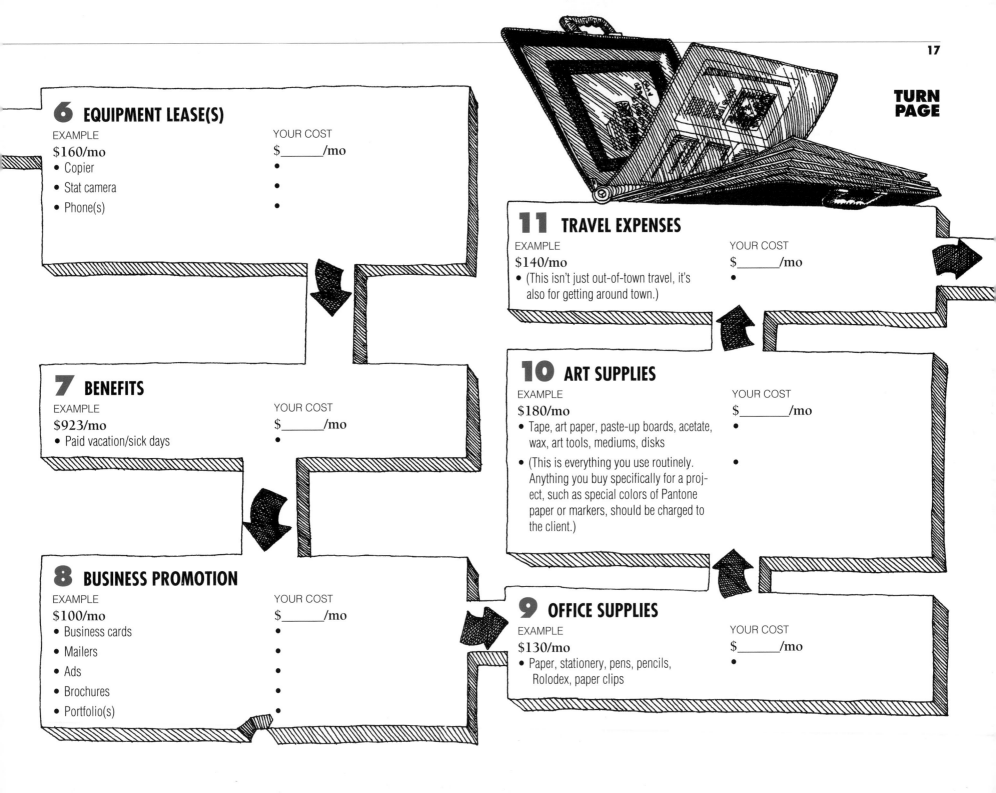

6 EQUIPMENT LEASE(S)

EXAMPLE
$160/mo
- Copier
- Stat camera
- Phone(s)

YOUR COST
$_____/mo
-
-
-

7 BENEFITS

EXAMPLE
$923/mo
- Paid vacation/sick days

YOUR COST
$_____/mo
-

8 BUSINESS PROMOTION

EXAMPLE
$100/mo
- Business cards
- Mailers
- Ads
- Brochures
- Portfolio(s)

YOUR COST
$_____/mo
-
-
-
-
-

11 TRAVEL EXPENSES

EXAMPLE
$140/mo
- (This isn't just out-of-town travel, it's also for getting around town.)

YOUR COST
$_____/mo
-

10 ART SUPPLIES

EXAMPLE
$180/mo
- Tape, art paper, paste-up boards, acetate, wax, art tools, mediums, disks
- (This is everything you use routinely. Anything you buy specifically for a project, such as special colors of Pantone paper or markers, should be charged to the client.)

YOUR COST
$_____/mo
-
-

9 OFFICE SUPPLIES

EXAMPLE
$130/mo
- Paper, stationery, pens, pencils, Rolodex, paper clips

YOUR COST
$_____/mo
-

WORKSHEET 3 *CONTINUED*

16 SAVINGS FOR RETIREMENT: ADD $166.67/MO TO AMOUNT IN BOX 15

EXAMPLE
$12,986.34/mo
($12,653.00 + 333.34)
• (If you both want to make a yearly contribution to IRAs or other type of retirement fund, $166.67/mo apiece falls safely within the maximum you can put aside.)

YOUR COST
$_____/mo
•

12 BUSINESS ENTERTAINMENT

EXAMPLE
$80/mo

YOUR COST
$_____/mo

15 TOTAL BOXES 1–14 TO GET YOUR BASIC MONTHLY OPERATING COSTS

EXAMPLE
$12,653.00/mo

YOUR COST
$_____/mo

13 EQUIPMENT PURCHASES

EXAMPLE
$700/mo
• (This is usually part of your start-up costs and stays roughly the same after the first year. Budget at least a small amount for replacement or additions if you have no ongoing expenses. I figured this on an initial outlay of $7,200, broken into monthly payments.)
• Computer
• Fax machine
• Printer
• Waxer
• Light box

YOUR COST
$_____/mo
•

•
•
•
•
•

14 FURNITURE PURCHASES

EXAMPLE
$500/mo
• (This is figured on the same basis as equipment—an initial outlay of $6,000, broken into monthly payments.)
• Desk
• Chair(s)
• Drawing board
• Table(s)
• Computer stand
• Printer stand
• Bulletin board

YOUR COST
$_____/mo
•

•
•
•
•
•
•
•

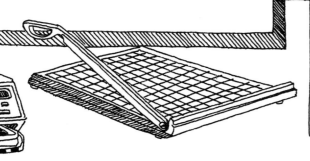

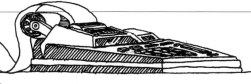

17 MULTIPLY THE TOTAL IN BOX 16 BY 10-20%, IF YOU WANT TO MAKE A PROFIT

EXAMPLE
$1,947.95/mo
($12,986.34 x .15(15%))

• (If you want to make any profit beyond your salary and retirement fund contribution, you have to figure that into your rate. It's not really an expense, but it's best to include it here.)

YOUR COST
$_____/mo

•

18 ADD BOXES 16 AND 17 TO GET YOUR TOTAL MONTHLY OPERATING COSTS

EXAMPLE
$14,934.29/mo

YOUR COST
$_____/mo

19 DIVIDE THE TOTAL IN BOX 18 BY 4 TO GET YOUR WEEKLY OPERATING COSTS

EXAMPLE
$3,733.57/wk
($14,934.29 / 4)

• (That's 4 for 4 weeks/month)
• (4 weeks per month is used because 48 working weeks per year is what you'll realistically average. That allows for 4 weeks of vacation, sick days and holidays—the yearly average taken by most self-employed designers.)

YOUR COST
$_____/wk

•

•

20 DIVIDE THE AMOUNT IN BOX 19 BY 5 TO GET YOUR DAILY OPERATING COSTS

EXAMPLE
$746.71/day
($3,733.57 / 5)

• (That's 5 for 5 work days in a week.)

YOUR COST
$_____/day

•

21 DIVIDE THE AMOUNT IN BOX 20 BY 6 TO GET YOUR HOURLY RATE: $62.23/HR

EXAMPLE
• Round that amount up or down to the nearest even dollar to get your Hourly Rate...$62/hr

• (That's 12 for 6 billable hours apiece in the average work day. Although you may both be in the studio every day for at least 8 hours, you'll probably never come up with more than 6 hours per day that you can actually bill to a client.)

• If you want to see the results of working fewer days or hours per week, simply plug those numbers into Boxes 19 and 20.

YOUR COST
$_____/hr

•

•

GOAL

WORKSHEET 4
YOU ARE A DESIGNER WITH TWO STAFFERS

This worksheet covers expenses for you and a staff of 2 full-time designers. Salaries vary with experience (more experienced, higher paid). Clerical staff generally receives lower salaries than design associates. Having part-time staff cuts costs. To know what hourly fees you need to charge to pay your bills and make money, too, fill in the requested dollar amounts as you move through the gameboard. Skip boxes that do not apply, but otherwise go in order. This worksheet has been filled in to show you what a sheet for someone like you would look like.

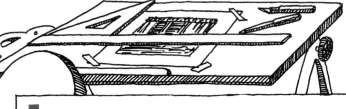

5 INSURANCE

EXAMPLE
$1,400/mo
YOUR COST
$_____/mo
- Health/equipment/business/premises
-
- (Because you would most likely have a group plan, include costs for employee health insurance here, rather than under benefits.)
-

START

1 YOUR STUDIO RENT

EXAMPLE
$1,100/mo
YOUR COST
$_____/mo
- (This is for a studio outside the home. If you are working out of your home, you should still charge yourself rent—a percentage equal to the percentage of your home that you use.)
-

4 TAXES

EXAMPLE
$4,200/mo
YOUR COST
$_____/mo
- Business/self-employment taxes (if not incorporated)/payroll taxes on employees (FICA, TDI, Social Security)/sales tax
-

2 SALARIES—YOURSELF PLUS YOUR 2 STAFFERS

EXAMPLE
$7,750/mo
YOUR COST
$_____/mo
- ($42,000/yr for you, $27,000/yr for one designer, and $24,000/yr for the other. If you anticipate hiring someone within a budget year, use a percentage of a year's salary; e.g., a half year's work equals a half year's salary.)
-

3 UTILITIES

EXAMPLE
$360/mo
YOUR COST
$_____/mo
- Electric
- Heat
- Air conditioning
- Phone
-
-
-
-

**TURN
PAGE**

6 EQUIPMENT LEASE(S)

EXAMPLE
$300/mo
YOUR COST
$_____/mo

- Fax
- Copier
- Stat camera
- Phones

- •
- •
- •
- •

7 BENEFITS

EXAMPLE
$1,789/mo
YOUR COST
$_____/mo

- Paid vacations/sick days
  (This assumes you and your associates
  each have two weeks of vacation. A new
  employee might get only one week.)
- Company car

- •

- •

8 BUSINESS PROMOTION

EXAMPLE
$200/mo
YOUR COST
$_____/mo

- Business cards
- Mailers
- Brochures
- Portfolio

- •
- •
- •
- •

11 TRAVEL EXPENSES

EXAMPLE
$250/mo
YOUR COST
$_____/mo

- (This is not just long distance but also
  local travel.)

- •

10 ART SUPPLIES

EXAMPLE
$350/mo
YOUR COST
$_____/mo

- Paste-up boards
- Wax
- Art tools
- Tape, acetate
- Computer disks

- •
- •
- •
- •
- •

9 OFFICE SUPPLIES

EXAMPLE
$275/mo
YOUR COST
$_____/mo

- Paper
- Stationery
- Pens
- Pencils
- Rolodex

- •
- •
- •
- •
- •

WORKSHEET 4 *CONTINUED*

12 BUSINESS ENTERTAINMENT

EXAMPLE
$120/mo
• (This assumes that the staffers aren't entertaining clients. Otherwise it would be higher.)

YOUR COST
$_____/mo
•

13 EQUIPMENT PURCHASES

EXAMPLE
$1,000/mo
• (This usually stays roughly the same for several years, but adding staff often means adding equipment. Always budget an amount to cover repair, replacement and additions.)
• Computers/printer(s)
• Fax machine
• Light boxes
• Waxer

YOUR COST
$_____/mo
•
•
•
•
•

16 MULTIPLY $166.67/MO BY THE NUMBER OF PEOPLE FOR WHOM YOU WILL CONTRIBUTE TO A RETIREMENT FUND

EXAMPLE
$500.01/mo
• (Self and both staffers covered = $166.67 x 3)

YOUR COST
$_____/mo
•

15 TOTAL BOXES 1–14 TO GET YOUR BASIC MONTHLY OPERATING COSTS

EXAMPLE
$19,794/mo

YOUR COST
$_____/mo

14 FURNITURE PURCHASES

EXAMPLE
$700/mo
• (This usually stays roughly the same for several years. Each new employee, however, means more furniture. Always budget an amount to cover repair, replacement and additions.)
• Desks
• Drawing boards
• Computer stands

YOUR COST
$_____/mo
•
•
•
•

17 TOTAL BOXES 15 AND 16

EXAMPLE
$20,294.01/mo
(19,794 + 500.01)

YOUR COST
$_____/mo

18 MULTIPLY THE AMOUNT IN BOX 17 BY 10-20%, IF YOU WOULD LIKE TO MAKE A PROFIT ABOVE AND BEYOND YOUR SALARY AND RETIREMENT FUND CONTRIBUTION

EXAMPLE
$3,044.10/mo
($20,294.01 x .15 (15%))

YOUR COST
$_____/mo

19 TOTAL BOXES 17 AND 18 TO GET YOUR TOTAL

EXAMPLE
$23,338.11/mo

YOUR COST
$_____/mo

20 DIVIDE THE AMOUNT IN BOX 19 BY 4 (WEEKS) TO GET YOUR WEEKLY OPERATING COSTS

EXAMPLE
$5,834.53/wk
• (Using 4 wks/mo allows for 4 annual weeks of vacation, sick days and holidays for you and each staffer—the average taken.)

YOUR COST
$_____/wk
•

21 DIVIDE THE AMOUNT IN BOX 20 BY 5 (WORK DAYS/ WEEK) TO GET YOUR DAILY OPERATING COSTS

EXAMPLE
$1,166.91/day

YOUR COST
$_____/day

22 MULTIPLY 6 (BILLABLE HOURS) TIMES THE NUMBER OF STAFFERS AND ADD 4 HOURS FOR YOURSELF

EXAMPLE
16 hrs/day
• Although your staffers are in the studio every day for 8 hours, you'll probably never come up with more than 6 hours per day per person that you can bill to a client. If design staffers are also doing clerical work, you may want to use 5 hours per day.)

YOUR HOURS
_____hrs/day
•

23 DIVIDE THE AMOUNT IN BOX 21 BY 16 (WORK HOURS PER DAY) TO GET YOUR HOURLY RATE

GOAL

EXAMPLE
$72.93/hr
• Round that amount up or down to the nearest even dollar amount to get your Hourly Rate...........................$73/hr
• (If you charge less for work by your assistants than for work you do, consider charging more than this Hourly Rate for your own services. Remember that the Hourly Rate is what you must make in order to meet expenses and earn a profit.)

YOUR COST
$_____/hr
•

•

WORKSHEET 5

YOU HAVE A STUDIO WITH A STAFF OF FIVE

This worksheet includes expenses for a studio outside the home with a full-time staff of 5: 2 designers, a junior designer, an assistant designer and a secretary. Salaries and benefits would be less for any part-time staff. To know what hourly fees you need to charge to pay bills and make money, too, fill in the requested dollar amounts as you move through the gameboard. Skip boxes that do not apply, but otherwise go in order. This worksheet has been filled in to show you what a sheet for someone like you would look like.

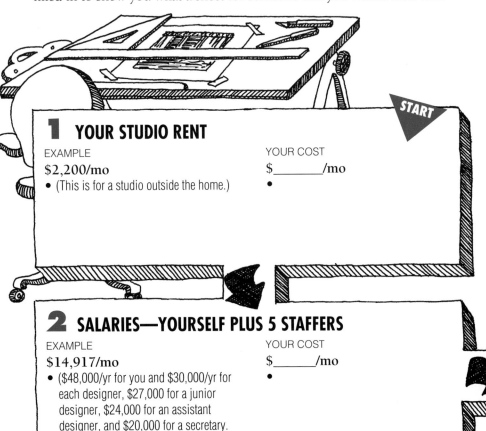

START

1 YOUR STUDIO RENT

EXAMPLE
$2,200/mo
• (This is for a studio outside the home.)

YOUR COST
$_____/mo
•

2 SALARIES—YOURSELF PLUS 5 STAFFERS

EXAMPLE
$14,917/mo
• ($48,000/yr for you and $30,000/yr for each designer, $27,000 for a junior designer, $24,000 for an assistant designer, and $20,000 for a secretary. If you anticipate hiring someone within your budget year, use a percentage of a year's salary.)

YOUR COST
$_____/mo
•

5 INSURANCE

EXAMPLE
$2,800/mo
• Health/equipment/business/premises
• (Because you would most likely have a group plan, include costs for employee health insurance here, rather than under benefits.)

YOUR COST
$_____/mo
•
•

4 TAXES

EXAMPLE
$8,000/mo
• Business/self-employment taxes (if not incorporated)/payroll taxes on employees (FICA, TDI, Social Security)/sales tax

YOUR COST
$_____/mo
•

3 UTILITIES

EXAMPLE
$720/mo
• Electric
• Heat
• Air conditioning
• Phone

YOUR COST
$_____/mo
•
•
•
•

TURN PAGE

6 EQUIPMENT LEASE(S)

EXAMPLE

$500/mo
- Computer
- Copier
- Stat camera
- Phone(s)

YOUR COST

$_____/mo
- •
- •
- •
- •

7 BENEFITS

EXAMPLE

$6,885/mo
- Paid vacations/sick days
  (This assumes you and your associates each have 2 weeks of vacation. A new employee might get only 1 week.)
- Car

YOUR COST

$_____/mo
- •

- •

8 BUSINESS PROMOTION

EXAMPLE

$250/mo
- Business cards
- Mailers
- Brochures
- Portfolio

YOUR COST

$_____/mo
- •
- •
- •
- •

11 TRAVEL EXPENSES

EXAMPLE

$400/mo
- (This is not just long distance but also local travel.)

YOUR COST

$_____/mo
- •

10 ART SUPPLIES

EXAMPLE

$1,000/mo
- Paste-up boards
- Wax
- Art tools
- Tape, acetate
- Computer disks

YOUR COST

$_____/mo
- •
- •
- •
- •
- •

9 OFFICE SUPPLIES

EXAMPLE

$550/mo
- Paper
- Stationery
- Pens
- Pencils
- Rolodex

YOUR COST

$_____/mo
- •
- •
- •
- •
- •

WORKSHEET 5 CONTINUED

12 BUSINESS ENTERTAINMENT

EXAMPLE
$240/mo
• (This assumes that not all staffers entertain clients. Otherwise it would be higher.)

YOUR COST
$_____/mo
•

13 EQUIPMENT PURCHASES

EXAMPLE
$2,000/mo
• (This usually stays roughly the same for several years, but adding staff often means adding equipment. Always budget an amount to cover repair, replacement and additions.)

• Computers/printers
• Fax machine
• Waxer
• Light table(s)

YOUR COST
$_____/mo
•

•
•
•
•

16 MULTIPLY $166.67/MO BY THE NUMBER OF PEOPLE FOR WHOM YOU WILL CONTRIBUTE TO A RETIREMENT FUND

EXAMPLE
$1,002.02/mo
• (Self and 5 staffers covered = $166.67 x 6)

YOUR COST
$_____/mo
•

15 TOTAL BOXES 1–14 TO GET YOUR BASIC MONTHLY OPERATING COSTS

EXAMPLE
$41,862/mo

YOUR COST
$_____/mo

14 FURNITURE PURCHASES

EXAMPLE
$1,400/mo
• (This usually stays roughly the same for several years. Each new employee, however, means more furniture. Always budget an amount to cover repair, replacement and additions.)

• Desks
• Drawing boards
• Computer stands

YOUR COST
$_____/mo
•

•
•
•

17 TOTAL BOXES 15 AND 16

EXAMPLE
$42,862.02/mo
($41,862.00 + 1,000.02)

YOUR COST
$_____/mo

18 MULTIPLY THE AMOUNT IN BOX 17 BY 10-20% , IF YOU WOULD LIKE TO MAKE A PROFIT ABOVE AND BEYOND YOUR SALARY AND RETIREMENT FUND CONTRIBUTION

EXAMPLE
$6,429.30/mo
($42,862.02 x .15 (15%))

YOUR COST
$_____/mo

19 TOTAL BOXES 17 AND 18 TO GET YOUR TOTAL MONTHLY OPERATING COSTS

EXAMPLE
$49,291.32/mo

YOUR COST
$_____/mo

20 DIVIDE THE AMOUNT IN BOX 19 BY 4 (WEEKS) TO GET YOUR WEEKLY OPERATING COSTS

EXAMPLE
$12,322.83/wk
• (Using 4 wks/mo allows for 4 annual weeks of vacation, sick days and holidays for you and each staffer—the average taken.)

YOUR COST
$_____/wk
•

23 DIVIDE THE AMOUNT IN BOX 21 BY 28 (WORK HOURS PER DAY) TO GET YOUR HOURLY RATE

EXAMPLE
$88.02/hr
• Round that amount up or down to the nearest even dollar amount to get your Hourly Rate..............................$88/hr
• (If you charge less for work by your assistants than for work you do, consider charging more than this Hourly Rate for your own services. Remember that the Hourly Rate is what you must make in order to meet expenses and earn a profit.)

YOUR COST
$_____/hr
•

•

22 MULTIPLY 6 (BILLABLE HOURS) TIMES THE NUMBER OF STAFFERS AND ADD 4 HOURS FOR YOURSELF

EXAMPLE
28 hrs/day
• Although your staffers are in the studio every day for 8 hours, you'll probably never come up with more than 6 hours per day per person that you can bill to a client. None of the secretary's time is billable; it's all overhead for you.
• (You have fewer billable hours because you're supervising the staffers.)

YOUR HOURS
_____hrs/day
•

•

21 DIVIDE THE AMOUNT IN BOX 20 BY 5 (WORK DAYS/WEEK) TO GET YOUR DAILY OPERATING COSTS

EXAMPLE
$2,464.57/day

YOUR COST
$_____/day

GOAL

WORKSHEET 6

YOU HAVE A STUDIO WITH A STAFF OF TEN

This worksheet includes expenses for a studio with 10 full-time staff, ranging from a senior designer to several junior designers and a secretary. Salaries and benefits would be lower for part-time employees. To know what hourly fees to charge to pay bills and make money, too, fill in the requested dollar amounts as you move through the gameboard. Skip boxes that do not apply, but otherwise go in order. This worksheet has been filled in to show you what a sheet for someone like you would look like.

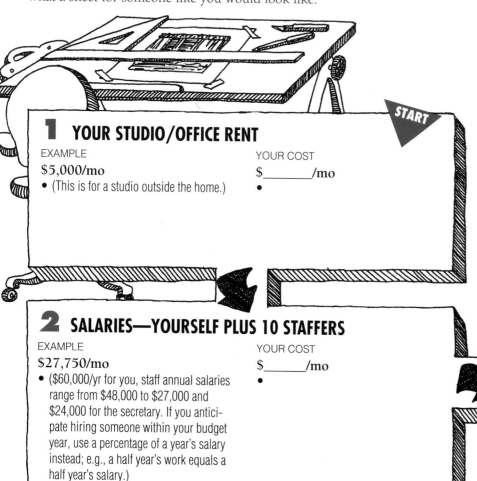

START

1 YOUR STUDIO/OFFICE RENT

EXAMPLE
$5,000/mo
• (This is for a studio outside the home.)

YOUR COST
$_____/mo
•

2 SALARIES—YOURSELF PLUS 10 STAFFERS

EXAMPLE
$27,750/mo
• ($60,000/yr for you, staff annual salaries range from $48,000 to $27,000 and $24,000 for the secretary. If you anticipate hiring someone within your budget year, use a percentage of a year's salary instead; e.g., a half year's work equals a half year's salary.)

YOUR COST
$_____/mo
•

5 INSURANCE

EXAMPLE
$7,000/mo
• Health/equipment/business/premises
• (Because you would most likely have a group plan, include costs for employee health insurance here, rather than under benefits.)

YOUR COST
$_____/mo
•
•

4 TAXES

EXAMPLE
$18,000/mo
• Business/self-employment taxes (if not incorporated)/payroll taxes on employees (FICA, TDI, Social Security)/sales tax

YOUR COST
$_____/mo
•

3 UTILITIES

EXAMPLE
$1,440/mo
• Electric
• Heat
• Air conditioning
• Phone

YOUR COST
$_____/mo
•
•
•
•

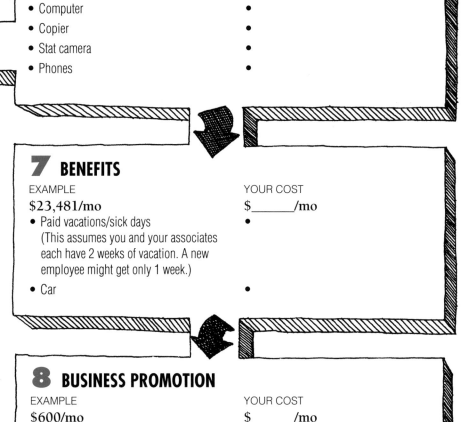

TURN PAGE

6 EQUIPMENT LEASE(S)

EXAMPLE	YOUR COST
$800/mo	**$_____/mo**
• Computer	•
• Copier	•
• Stat camera	•
• Phones	•

11 TRAVEL EXPENSES

EXAMPLE	YOUR COST
$800/mo	**$_____/mo**
• (This is not just long distance but also local travel.)	•

7 BENEFITS

EXAMPLE	YOUR COST
$23,481/mo	**$_____/mo**
• Paid vacations/sick days (This assumes you and your associates each have 2 weeks of vacation. A new employee might get only 1 week.)	•
• Car	•

10 ART SUPPLIES

EXAMPLE	YOUR COST
$2,000/mo	**$_____/mo**
• Paste-up boards	•
• Wax	•
• Art tools	•
• Tape, acetate	•
• Computer disks	•

8 BUSINESS PROMOTION

EXAMPLE	YOUR COST
$600/mo	**$_____/mo**
• Business cards	•
• Mailers	•
• Brochures	•
• Portfolio	•

9 OFFICE SUPPLIES

EXAMPLE	YOUR COST
$1,100/mo	**$_____/mo**
• Paper	•
• Stationery	•
• Pens	•
• Pencils	•
• Rolodex	•

WORKSHEET 6 *CONTINUED*

12 BUSINESS ENTERTAINMENT

EXAMPLE
$480/mo
• (This assumes that not all staffers entertain clients. Otherwise it would be higher.)

YOUR COST
$_____/mo
•

13 EQUIPMENT PURCHASES

EXAMPLE
$6,000/mo
• (This usually stays roughly the same for several years, but adding staff often means adding equipment. Always budget an amount to cover repair, replacement and additions.)
• Computers/printer(s)
• Fax machine
• Light boxes
• Waxer

YOUR COST
$_____/mo
•
•
•
•
•

16 MULTIPLY $166.67/MO BY THE NUMBER OF PEOPLE FOR WHOM YOU WILL CONTRIBUTE TO A RETIREMENT FUND

EXAMPLE
$1,833.37/mo
• (Self and 10 staffers covered = $166.67 x 11)

YOUR COST
$_____/mo
•

15 TOTAL BOXES 1–14 TO GET YOUR BASIC MONTHLY OPERATING COSTS

EXAMPLE
$97,451/mo

YOUR COST
$_____/mo

14 FURNITURE PURCHASES

EXAMPLE
$3,000/mo
• (This usually stays roughly the same for several years. Each new employee, however, means more furniture. Always budget an amount to cover repair, replacement and additions.)
• Desks
• Drawing boards
• Computer stands

YOUR COST
$_____/mo
•
•
•
•

17 TOTAL BOXES 15 AND 16

EXAMPLE
$99,284.37/mo
($97,451 + 1,833.37)

YOUR COST
$_____/mo

18 MULTIPLY THE AMOUNT IN BOX 17 BY 10-20%, IF YOU WOULD LIKE TO MAKE A PROFIT ABOVE AND BEYOND YOUR SALARY AND RETIREMENT FUND CONTRIBUTION

EXAMPLE
$14,892.66/mo
($99,284.37 x .15 (15%))

YOUR COST
$_____/mo

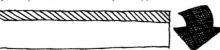

19 TOTAL BOXES 17 AND 18 TO GET YOUR TOTAL MONTHLY OPERATING COSTS

EXAMPLE
$114,177.03/mo

YOUR COST
$_____/mo

20 DIVIDE THE AMOUNT IN BOX 19 BY 4 (WEEKS) TO GET YOUR WEEKLY OPERATING COSTS

EXAMPLE
$28,544.26/wk

YOUR COST
$_____/wk

- (Using 4 wks/mo allows for 4 annual weeks of vacation, sick days and holidays for you and each staffer—the average taken.)

23 DIVIDE THE AMOUNT IN BOX 21 BY 55 (WORK HOURS PER DAY) TO GET YOUR HOURLY RATE

EXAMPLE
$103.80/hr
- Round that amount up or down to the nearest even dollar amount to get your Hourly Rate...........................$104/hr
- (If you charge less for work by junior designers than for work you or senior designers do, consider charging more than this Hourly Rate for your own services. That Hourly Rate is what you must make in order to meet expenses and earn a profit.)

YOUR COST
$_____/hr
-
-

22 MULTIPLY 6 (BILLABLE HOURS) TIMES THE 8 DESIGNERS, AND ADD 4 HOURS FOR THE SENIOR DESIGNER AND 3 HOURS FOR YOURSELF

EXAMPLE
55 hrs/day
- Although your staffers are in the studio for 8 hours, you'll probably get 6 hours per day per person that you can bill to a client. None of the secretary's time is billable; it's all overhead for you.
- (You and the senior designer have fewer billable hours because you're supervising the others.)

YOUR HOURS
_____hrs/day
-
-

21 DIVIDE THE AMOUNT IN BOX 20 BY 5 (WORK DAYS/WEEK) TO GET YOUR DAILY OPERATING COSTS

EXAMPLE
$5,708.85/day

YOUR COST
$_____/day

Pricing Design & Illustration Projects

These worksheets, in an easy-to-use gameboard format, show how to price common design and illustration projects. Find the worksheet that most closely matches your project, then follow the boxes to work out the pricing. The example in each box lists factors that can affect the cost of a design or illustration project.

Use quotes from your own vendors and develop your own estimates of how many hours each stage will take. The figures given as examples here are only generic estimates of time and costs; they are not intended to represent exactly how long a project should take or what materials and services will cost. An hourly rate of $60/hour has been used for all examples in the worksheets.

Worksheet examples for illustration projects typically given on a flat fee basis show how to determine if you will actually make any money—or at least break even. The difference between your time costs plus expenses and the budget for the job is used as the usage fee earned on that job. The usage fee, therefore, does not necessarily represent the "right" or ideal charge for a particular project.

To clearly illustrate the difference rush charges can make in pricing a project, rush charges are figured in a separate box, Urgency of Job, and

added onto existing hours. Since total hours have been calculated on the worksheet by the time you reach this box, only the additional charge for any overtime is added. For example, a project will take 161 hours; at $60/hour that will cost the client $9,660. Of those 161 hours, 35 will be overtime; another $30/hour in overtime charges for each of those 35 hours is now added. In other words, at $60/hour time-and-a-half is $90/hour. Since you've already calculated the $60/hour part in the worksheet, you will add on only the extra $30/hour.

A percentage of the total charge for the job can also be charged as a rush charge fee. Rush charge percentages can range from 5% to 100% on projects with overly tight deadlines. For example, a rush job will take 161 hours at $60/hour for a total cost of $9,660. Now, a typical rush charge of 20% will be added. Add $1,932 ($9,660 x .2) for a total time cost of $11,592.

Most of the entries in the boxes can be transferred to the actual cost estimate you give a client. Three boxes, however, would not be broken out as line items on an estimate—Complexity of Job, Client Requirements for the Project and Hidden Surprise Factor. Complexity of Job provides a margin for intangibles often overlooked when calculat-

ing the hours needed to complete a job. Client Requirements for the Project covers high quality output or similar factors can result in a job taking longer than you can easily anticipate. On a cost estimate you would add the hours for Complexity of Job and Client Requirements to those under the most appropriate heading. For example, if you had quite a few hours budgeted in Complexity of Job because there was a large number of photos to be handled, you would add the extra hours for Complexity of Job between Client Meetings and Mechanical Preparation.

The Hidden Surprise Factor box tells you how many hours you should pad your estimate to guard against unanticipated problems. For example, you're bidding on what should be a simple letterhead and planning to output from disk directly to film. Adding a reasonable 5% margin as a Hidden Surprise Factor covers you if your page layout program suddenly decides not to accept the artwork you created in your drawing program and you have to fix the problem or rebuild the file. Divide that number by the number of categories or phases in the estimate and add the same amount to each. (Do the same thing with the Margin for Extra Costs entry included in the Production Costs box.)

WORKSHEET 7
LOGO/LETTERHEAD/IDENTITY SYSTEM

This worksheet can be used to estimate the cost of a logo design, a letterhead design, an identity system design, or any combination of the above. The example here is based on a project where you design a logo and an identity system with only a few applications.

Accurately estimating the cost of any project involves figuring out the cost of the materials and services you'll purchase on behalf of the client as well as the cost of your time. To arrive at an estimate for a job, fill in the amounts requested as you move through the gameboard. Skip boxes that do not apply, but otherwise go in order until you reach the goal. Inside each box you'll find an example printed on the left and blank spaces on the right for you to use.

START

1 PROJECT TITLE— DESIGN LOGO & IDENTITY SYSTEM

Client Name: TechCom Corporation
Client Budget: $21,000-23,000
Time Frame: 2 months

2 COMPLEXITY OF JOB

EXAMPLE
What We Know:
- This is a new logo for an existing company
- For letterheads, business cards, folders and product sheets
- Client is demanding
- Extensive research of competitive identity systems
- Contract must clearly state kill fee
- Deadline is tight—requires some overtime
- Time needed..................................4 hrs

Total Time Required ....4 hrs

YOUR HOURS
What You Know:
-
-
-
-
-
-
- Time needed ...._____hrs

Total Time Required.............._____hrs

4 CONCEPT DEVELOPMENT

EXAMPLE
What We Know:
- Client wants 10-20 roughs of logo concepts
- Add revision time for finalizing client's selection
- Client wants 3-5 applications roughs of chosen concept
- Time needed ....55 hrs

What We Need:
- Survey of personnel on logo requirements
- Marketing studies on current logo
- Time needed ....17 hrs

Total Time Required ....72 hrs

YOUR HOURS
What You Know:
-
-
-
- Time needed ...._____hrs

What You Need:
-
-
- Time needed ...._____hrs

Total Time Required ...._____hrs

3 INITIAL CLIENT MEETING

EXAMPLE
What We Know:
- Client wants to have lots of input throughout process
- Time needed ....3 hrs

What We Need:
- General info on competitors' logos
- Info on TechCom and its market
- Concepts developed by last design firm
- Time needed ....3 hrs

Total Time Required ....6 hrs

YOUR HOURS
What You Know:
-
- Time needed ...._____hrs

What You Need:
-
-
-
- Time needed ...._____hrs

Total Time Required ...._____hrs

5 CLIENT REQUIREMENTS FOR PROJECT

EXAMPLE

What We Know:
- Highly sophisticated logo with strong corporate look
- High-end production required
- Lots of top management involved
- Concept must be distinctively different from competitors
- Must research competitors' stationery, etc.
- Time needed ....15 hrs

Total Time Required ....**15 hrs**

YOUR HOURS

What You Know:
-
-
-
-
-
- Time needed ...._____hrs

Total Time Required ...._____hrs

TURN PAGE

8 CLIENT MEETINGS

EXAMPLE

What We Know:
- Meeting to discuss survey results
- Two rounds of meetings on roughs
- Meeting to approve mechanicals/comps
- Time needed ....13 hrs

What We Need:
- Approval/change forms for client signature
- Limits on rounds of revisions before additional charges begin
- Time needed ....1 hr

Total Time Required.........14 hrs

YOUR HOURS

What You Know:
-
-
-
- Time needed ...._____hrs

What You Need:
-
-
- Time needed ...._____hrs

Total Time Required....____hrs

6 PREPARING COMPS

EXAMPLE

What We Know:
- Develop color comps of logo to show placement on stationery, business card, envelopes, product sheets and folders
- Presenting system to board of directors/top management
- Client expects slick presentation
- Time needed ....13 hrs

What We Need:
- Presentation packets for participants
- Color copies of logo applications for presentation packets
- Extra rehearsal time
- Time needed ....30 hrs

Total Time Required ....**43 hrs**

YOUR HOURS

What You Know:
-
-
-
- Time needed ...._____hrs

What You Need:
-
-
-
- Time needed ...._____hrs

Total Time Required ...._____hrs

7 MECHANICAL PREPARATION

EXAMPLE

What We Know:
- Send disk with logo applications to service bureau for high-resolution output
- Typesetting with final revisions to be done
- Design is 2-color and embossed— prepare overlays
- Prepare and proof boards for 15 pieces
- Time needed ....52 hrs

What We Need:
- Artwork for emboss
- Request bids (prices/schedules) from vendors/subcontractors
- In-house production schedule
- Time needed ....7 hrs

Total Time Required ....59 hrs

YOUR HOURS

What You Know:
-
-
-
- Time needed ...._____hrs

What You Need:
-
-
- Time needed ...._____hrs

Total Time Required...____hrs

WORKSHEET 7 CONTINUED

9 CLERICAL/ADMINISTRATIVE WORK

EXAMPLE

What We Know:
- Prepare price estimate and schedule
- Set up billing account
- Time needed ....3 hrs

What We Need:
- Bid confirmations from vendors/subcontractors
- Time needed ....1 hr

Total Time Required ....4 hrs

YOUR HOURS

What You Know:
-
-
- Time needed..............._____hrs

What You Need:
-
- Time needed..............._____hrs

Total Time Required ...._____hrs

10 TOTAL PROJECT HOURS

EXAMPLE
- Total Boxes 1-9 to estimate Total Project Hours...217 hrs
  (If you charge different rates for activities, divide the box into sections, one section per rate. For example, if you have the same rate for Comp and for Mechanical Prep, assign one section of the box for those total hours.)

YOUR HOURS
-

12 TIME COSTS

EXAMPLE
- Multiply the total number of project hours in Box 11 by your Hourly Fee Rate to get the Total Project Time Costs.......$15,000
  (To simplify the example, an average hourly fee of $60 has been used. If you charge different rates for activities, multiply the hours for all activities for which you charge the same rate by that rate. Total all the charges. For example, Concept Development + Client Meetings = 70 hrs x $85/hr = $5,950)

YOUR COSTS
-

11 HIDDEN SURPRISE FACTOR

EXAMPLE
- Multiply the amount in Box 10 by .15 (15%); add that to Box 10 to guard against hidden surprises (accidents, emergencies, problems caused by the client, etc.).................217 + 33 = 250 hrs
  (Build a margin into your estimate to avoid cost overruns that anger clients or cost you money. The hidden surprise factor used here is 15% because this client is clearly going to be difficult to work with; it's also a good idea to go to this level on a project you've never done before. A 5% security blanket may be enough in many cases.)

YOUR HOURS
-

13 URGENCY OF JOB

EXAMPLE
What We Know:
- Deadline is tight, requires overtime
- Time needed ....15 hrs
- Rush charge $30/hr

Total Time Required/Total Rush Costs........................15 hrs/$450
- (For a rush project, add your overtime charge or percentage for rush work. Enter here only the cost of the extra charge. For example, at $60, time-and-a-half would cost an extra $30/hour. For 3 hours of overtime, the charge would be $90. If the Total Project Time Cost was $1,200 and your rush charge percentage was 20%, a rush charge on the job would be $240 ($1,200 x .2))

YOUR COSTS
What You Know:
-
- Time needed ...._____hrs
- Rush charge..................$_____/hr

Total Time Required/Total Rush Costs...._____hrs/$_____
-

14 PRODUCTION COSTS

EXAMPLE
What We Know:
- Service bureau output $450
- Printing...2,075
- Embossing...800
- Stats...200
- Supplies...150
- Subtotal $3,675
- Markup (20%) 735

  (Not all artists charge markup; whether you do or don't, be consistent in your practice.)
- Total Known Costs.........................$4,410

What We Need:
- 5% margin for extra costs................$221

Total Production Costs..............................$4,631

YOUR COSTS
What You Know:
-
-
-
-
-
-
-
- Total Known Costs............$_____

What You Need:
-

Total Production Costs ....$_____

16 TOTAL PROJECT COSTS

EXAMPLE
What We Know:
- Total Project Costs...................$20,081
- Client wants all rights, plus copyright..............................$2,000 usage fee

Total Costs $22,081
- (Because a logo design is so specific to a client, it's often worthwhile to sell all rights, including the copyright, for a higher fee. Negotiate the amount with the client and expect it to vary from project to project. In these cases make sure the agreement spells out your right to use the logo and system design for self-promotion.)
- Sales Tax
  (Calculate sales tax only for the final invoice, since it has to be figured on actual costs.)

YOUR COSTS
What You Know:
-
-

Total Costs.................$_____
-

15 PRODUCTION AND FEE COSTS

EXAMPLE
- Total the dollar amounts in Boxes 12, 13 and 14 to get the total amount of service fees and production costs $20,081

YOUR COSTS
-

GOAL

WORKSHEET 8

2-COLOR BROCHURE, MODEST BUDGET

In this example, we'll look at a relatively simple self-mailer brochure for a nonprofit client. Worksheet 9 illustrates a more lavish brochure with a large budget.

Accurately estimating the cost of any project involves figuring out your time and the cost of materials and services you'll purchase on behalf of the client. To arrive at an estimate for a job, fill in the amounts requested as you move through the gameboard. Skip boxes that do not apply, but otherwise go in order until you reach the goal. Inside each box, you'll find an example printed on the left and blank spaces on the right for you to use.

START

1 TITLE— PROMOTIONAL/ SERVICE BROCHURE

Client Name: The Center for Women's Health
Client Budget: $7,000-10,000
Time Frame: 2 months

2 COMPLEXITY OF JOB

EXAMPLE | YOUR HOURS

What We Know:
- 2-color, self-mailing, 4-panel brochure
- Will use b&w photos or duotones
- Will include medical terminology
- Client supplying copy
- Previous brochures/promo material exist
- Time needed ....1 hr

What You Know:
-
-
-
-
-
- Time needed ...._____hrs

Total Time Required..............................1 hr

Total Time Required.............._____hrs

4 CONCEPT DEVELOPMENT

EXAMPLE | YOUR HOURS

What We Know:
- Make paper dummy to estimate mailing costs
- Show 1-2 roughs and type samples
- Add revision time for finalizing client selection
- Time needed ....20 hrs

What You Know:
-
-
-
- Time needed ...._____hrs

What We Need:
- Estimate of mailing cost
- Check folds with printer
- Time needed. ....7 hrs

What You Need:
-
-
- Time needed...................._____hrs

Total Time Required...........................27 hrs

Total Time Required ...._____hrs

3 INITIAL CLIENT MEETING

EXAMPLE | YOUR HOURS

What We Know:
- Discuss length and content of copy
- Determine number of photos and how supplied
- Time needed ....3 hrs

What You Know:
-
-
- Time needed ...._____hrs

What We Need:
- Client's existing photos
- Deadline for copy
- Time needed ....1 hr

What You Need:
-
-
- Time needed ...._____hrs

Total Time Required ....4 hrs

Total Time Required ...._____hrs

5 CLIENT REQUIREMENTS FOR PROJECT

EXAMPLE

What We Know:
- Keep production & mailing costs low
- Can't be slick, glossy or hard sell
- Photography must be low cost
- Time needed ....4 hrs

**Total Time
Required** ....4 hrs

YOUR HOURS

What You Know:
-
-
-
- Time needed ...._____hrs

**Total Time
Required** ...._____hrs

TURN PAGE

8 CLIENT MEETINGS

EXAMPLE

What We Know:
- Meet to approve roughs
- Meet to approve comps
- Meet to approve photos
- Time needed ....3 hrs

What We Need:
- Approval/change forms for client signature
- Time needed ....1 hr

**Total Time
Required** ....4 hrs

YOUR HOURS

What You Know:
-
-
-
- Time needed ...._____hrs

What You Need:
-
- Time needed ...._____hrs

**Total Time
Required**..................._____hrs

6 PREPARING COMPS

EXAMPLE

What We Know:
- Present concept to executive director/board of trustees
- Show paper dummy
- Show duotone samples from clip file
- Show sketch to illustrate color scheme
- Time needed ....10 hrs

What We Need:
- Samples of photographer's work
- Photocopies and greeked laser type
- Time needed ....2 hrs

**Total Time
Required** ....12 hrs

YOUR HOURS

What You Know:
-
-
-
-
- Time needed ...._____hrs

What You Need:
-
-
- Time needed ...._____hrs

**Total Time
Required**.............._____hrs

7 MECHANICAL PREPARATION

EXAMPLE

What We Know:
- Typesetting; final revisions done after client proofs boards
- 2-color design with duotones
- Prepare and proof boards
- Time needed ....20 hrs

What We Need:
- Request bids (prices/schedules) from vendors/subcontractors
- Arrange and oversee photo shoot
- Get photos approved by client
- Get halftones of photos
- Time needed ....10 hrs

**Total Time
Required** ....30 hrs

YOUR HOURS

What You Know:
-
-
- Time needed ...._____hrs

What You Need:
-
-
-
- Time needed ...._____hrs

**Total Time
Required**.............._____hrs

WORKSHEET 8 *CONTINUED*

9 CLERICAL/ADMINISTRATIVE WORK

EXAMPLE

What We Know:
- Prepare price estimate and schedule
- Set up billing account
- Time needed ....3 hrs

What We Need:
- Bid confirmation from all vendors/sub-contractors
- Time needed ....1 hr

Total Time Required ....4 hrs

YOUR HOURS

What You Know:
-
-
- Time needed ...._____hrs

What You Need:
-
- Time needed ...._____hrs

Total Time Required ...._____hrs

10 TOTAL PROJECT HOURS

EXAMPLE
- Total Boxes 1-9 to estimate Total Project Hours...86 hrs
  (If you charge different rates for activities, divide the box into sections, one section per rate. For example, if you use the same rate for Comp and for Mechanical Prep, assign one section of the box for those total hours.)

YOUR HOURS
-

12 TIME COSTS

EXAMPLE
- Multiply the total number of project hours in Box 11 by your Hourly Fee Rate to get the Total Project Time Costs......$5,700
  (To simplify the example, an average hourly fee of $60 has been used. If you charge different rates for activities, multiply the hours for all activities for which you charge the same rate by that rate. Total all the charges. For example, Concept Development + Client Meetings = 70 hrs x $85/hr = $5,950)

YOUR COSTS
-

11 HIDDEN SURPRISE FACTOR

EXAMPLE
- Multiply the amount in Box 10 by .10 (10%); add that to Box 10 to guard against hidden surprises (accidents, emergencies, problems caused by the client, etc.).......................86 + 9 = 95 hrs
  (Build a margin into your estimate to avoid cost overruns that anger clients or cost you money. The hidden surprise factor used here is 10% because there may be problems with the copy; the client is supplying it and medical terminology is involved. A 5% security blanket may be enough in many cases.)

YOUR HOURS
-

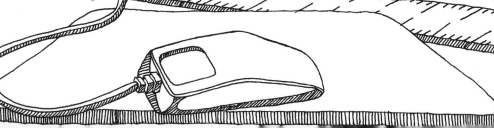

13 URGENCY OF JOB

EXAMPLE

What We Know:
- Deadline is manageable, no overtime
- Time needed ....0 hrs
- Rush charge. ....0%/$0

Total Time Required/Total Rush Costs.....................0 hrs/$0
- (For a rush project, add your overtime charge or percentage for rush work. Enter here only the cost of the extra charge. For example, at $60, time-and-a-half would cost an extra $30/hour. For 3 hours of overtime, the charge would be $90. If the Total Project Time Cost was $1,200 and your rush charge percentage was 20%, a rush charge on the job would be $240 ($1,200 x .2))

YOUR COSTS

What You Know:
-
- Time needed ...._____hrs
- Rush charge............_____%/$_____

Total Time Required/Total Rush Costs....._____hrs/$_____
-

16 TOTAL PROJECT COSTS

EXAMPLE

What We Know:
- Total Project Costs....................$8,023
- Client wants one-time rights, we keep originals ....$0 usage fee

Total Costs.....................$8,023
- (The more rights a client requests, the higher the fee you should charge. Be very careful if a client asks for "all rights" or a "buyout." The fee for the rights involved, if more than one-time rights, must be negotiated with the client and varies from project to project.)
- Sales Tax
  (Calculate sales tax only for the final invoice, since it has to be figured on actual costs.)

YOUR COSTS

What You Know:
-
-

Total Costs.................$_____
-

14 PRODUCTION COSTS

EXAMPLE

What We Know:
- Typesetting $200
- Printing...1,000
- Photography 500
- Stats..10
- Supplies...50
- Subtotal $1,760
- Markup (20%) 352
  (Not all artists charge markup; whether you do or don't, be consistent in your practice.)
- Total Known Costs........................$2,112

What We Need:
- 10% margin for extra costs..............$211

Total Production Costs...........................$2,323

YOUR COSTS

What You Know:
-
-
-
-
-
-
-
- Total Known Costs...............$_____

What You Need:
-

Total Production Costs..........................$_____

15 PRODUCTION AND FEE COSTS

EXAMPLE
- Total the dollar amounts in Boxes 12, 13 and 14 to get the total amount of service fees and production costs.............$8,023

YOUR COSTS
-

WORKSHEET 9
4-COLOR BROCHURE, HIGH BUDGET

This example illustrates a complex brochure project. The brochure will be heavily illustrated with 4-color photos that will be shot on location at 15 sites. A copywriter will produce the actual copy, which the client must approve.

Accurately estimating the cost of any project involves figuring out the cost of the materials and services you'll purchase on behalf of the client as well as the cost of your time. To arrive at an estimate for a job, fill in the amounts requested as you move through the gameboard. Skip boxes that do not apply, but otherwise go in order until you reach the goal. Inside each box you'll find an example printed on the left and blank spaces on the right for you to use.

START

1 PROJECT TITLE— CAPABILITIES BROCHURE

Client Name: CMS Air Cargo
Client Budget: $30,000-35,000
Time Frame: 1 month

2 COMPLEXITY OF JOB

EXAMPLE
What We Know:
- 4-color, 6-page brochure
- Flap for inserts, plus die-cut on flap for business card
- Photo shoots in 15 locations; company will fly photographer to sites
- Client has rough layout of brochure and Polaroids of sites/facilities
- Samples of competitive brochures are available
- Contract must clearly state kill fee
- Time needed ....3 hrs

Total Time Required..........3 hrs

YOUR HOURS
What You Know:
-
-
-
-
-
-
- Time needed ...._____hrs

Total Time Required....____hrs

4 CONCEPT DEVELOPMENT

EXAMPLE
What We Know:
- Client wants 3-5 layout roughs
- Client wants mock-ups in several paper stocks
- Present first draft of copy
- Time needed ....25 hrs

What We Need:
- Dummies weighed at post office to estimate mailing cost
- Envelope samples for dummies
- Time needed ....3 hrs

Total Time Required..........................28 hrs

YOUR HOURS
What You Know:
-
-
-
- Time needed ...._____hrs

What You Need:
-
-
- Time needed....................._____hrs

Total Time Required................._____hrs

3 INITIAL CLIENT MEETING

EXAMPLE
What We Know:
- Review client layouts and site Polaroids; make recommendations
- Discuss competitive brochures
- Time needed ....2 hrs

What We Need:
- Sample paper stocks
- Time needed ....1 hr

Total Time Required..........................3 hrs

YOUR HOURS
What You Know:
-
-
- Time needed ...._____hrs

What You Need:
-
- Time needed ...._____hrs

Total Time Required................._____hrs

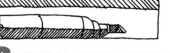

5 CLIENT REQUIREMENTS FOR PROJECT

EXAMPLE

What We Know:
- High quality product
- Extremely tight deadline
- Demanding client; expected to make many changes
- Presentation of designs to management
- Time needed ....15 hrs

Total Time Required..........................15 hrs

YOUR HOURS

What You Know:
-
-
-

- Time needed ...._____hrs

Total Time Required ...._____hrs

6 PREPARING COMPS

EXAMPLE

What We Know:
- Comp must be full color
- Copy to be revised
- Show photos in dummy
- Time needed ....15 hrs

What We Need:
- Samples of photographer's work
- Presentation packets for each manager
- Color copies of comp design
- Time needed ....5 hrs

Total Time Required............................20 hrs

YOUR HOURS

What You Know:
-
-
-

- Time needed ...._____hrs

What You Need:
-
-
-

- Time needed..................._____hrs

Total Time Required..............._____hrs

TURN PAGE

8 CLIENT MEETINGS

EXAMPLE

What We Know:
- Layout presentation
- Comp and copy approval; select photos
- Mechanical approval
- Approve revisions
- Time needed ....8 hrs

What We Need:
- Limit on rounds of revisions before additional charges begin
- Time needed ....1 hr

Total Time Required...........9 hrs

YOUR HOURS

What You Know:
-
-
-
-

- Time needed ...._____hrs

What You Need:
-

- Time needed ...._____hrs

Total Time Required..._____hrs

7 MECHANICAL PREPARATION

EXAMPLE

What We Know:
- Typesetting—final revisions done after client proofs boards
- Must prepare and proof boards
- Prepare photos for scanning
- Art direct photo shoot (15 sites/3 days)
- Must do press check
- Time needed..............................67 hrs

What We Need:
- Request bids (prices/schedules) from vendors/subcontractors
- Time needed...............................10 hrs

Total Time Required ....77 hrs

YOUR HOURS

What You Know:
-
-
-
-

- Time needed.................._____hrs

What You Need:
-

- Time needed.................._____hrs

Total Time Required ...._____hrs

WORKSHEET 9 CONTINUED

9 CLERICAL/ADMINISTRATIVE WORK

EXAMPLE | YOUR HOURS

What We Know:
- Prepare price estimate and schedule
- Set up billing account
- Time needed ....3 hrs

What You Know:
-
-
- Time needed................_____hrs

What We Need:
- Bid confirmation from vendors/subcontractors
- Time needed ....1 hr

What You Need:
-
- Time needed................_____hrs

Total Time Required ....4 hrs

Total Time Required ...._____hrs

10 TOTAL PROJECT HOURS

EXAMPLE
- Total Boxes 1-9 to estimate Total Project Hours...159 hrs
  (If you charge different rates for activities, divide the box into sections, one section per rate. For example, if you have the same rate for Comp and for Mechanical Prep, assign one section of the box for those total hours.)

YOUR HOURS
-

12 TIME COSTS

EXAMPLE
- Multiply the total number of project hours in Box 11 by your Hourly Fee Rate to get the Total Project Time Costs.......$11,460
  (To simplify the example, an average hourly fee of $60 was used. If you charge different rates for activities, multiply the hours for all activities for which you charge the same rate by that rate. Total all the charges. For example, Concept Development + Client Meetings = 70 hrs x $85/hr = $5,950)

YOUR COSTS
-

11 HIDDEN SURPRISE FACTOR

EXAMPLE
- Multiply the amount in Box 10 by .20 (20%); add that to Box 10 to guard against hidden surprises (accidents, emergencies, problems caused by the client, etc.)................159 + 32 = 191 hrs
  (Build a margin into your estimate to avoid cost overruns that anger clients or cost you money. In this case 20% is used because the client is expected to make many changes and time is of the essence.)

YOUR HOURS
-

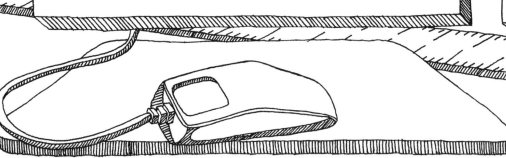

13 URGENCY OF JOB

EXAMPLE

What We Know:

- Rapid turnaround project requiring over-time

- Time needed ...._____

- Rush charge 15%

Total Time Required/Total Rush Costs ...._____/$1,719

- (For a rush project, add your overtime charge or percentage for rush work. Enter here only the cost of the extra charge. For example, at $60, time-and-a-half would cost an extra $30/hour. For 3 hours of overtime, the charge would be $90. If the Total Project Time Cost was $1,200 and your rush charge percentage was 20%, a rush charge on the job would be $240 ($1,200 x .2))

YOUR COSTS

What You Know:

-

- Time needed ...._____hrs

- Rush charge........................_____%

Total Time Required/Total Rush Costs.............._____hrs/$_____

-

14 PRODUCTION COSTS

EXAMPLE

What We Know:

- Typesetting $800

- Printing..7,500

- Photography 7,000

- Stats..450

- Supplies...250

- Copywriter 1,200

- Subtotal $17,200

- Markup (15%) 2,580

  (Not all artists charge markup; whether you do or don't, be consistent in your practice.)

- Total Known Costs......................$19,780

What We Need:

- 10% margin for extra costs..........$1,978

Total Production Costs $21,758

YOUR COSTS

What You Know:

-
-
-
-
-
-
-
-

- Total Known Costs..............$_____

What You Need:

-

Total Production Costs ....$_____

16 TOTAL PROJECT COSTS

EXAMPLE

What We Know:

- Total Project Costs..................$34,937

- Client is paying for one-time rights, we keep the originals...............$0 usage fee

Total Costs $34,937

- (The more rights a client requests, the higher the fee you should charge. Be very careful if a client asks for "all rights" or a "buyout." The fee for the rights involved, if more than one-time rights, must be negotiated with the client and varies from project to project.)

- Sales Tax
  (Calculate sales tax only for the final invoice since it has to be figured on actual costs.)

YOUR COSTS

What You Know:

-
-

Total Costs................$_____

-

-

15 PRODUCTION AND FEE COSTS

EXAMPLE

- Total the dollar amounts in Boxes 12, 13 and 14 to get the total amount of service fees and production costs $34,937

YOUR COSTS

-

WORKSHEET 10

BOOKLET DESIGN

This is an example of an instructional booklet where turnaround time is crucial. To save time, the booklet will be printed 4-color over 1-color and the client will supply the copy on disk.

Accurately estimating the cost of any project involves figuring out the cost of the materials and services you'll purchase on behalf of the client as well as the cost of your time. To arrive at an estimate for a job, fill in the amounts requested as you move through the game-board. Skip boxes that do not apply, but otherwise go in order until you reach the goal. Inside each box you'll find an example printed on the left and blank spaces on the right for you to use.

START

1 PROJECT TITLE— INSTRUCTIONAL BOOKLET DESIGN

Client Name: Prefab Furniture
  Manufacturer
Client Budget: $15,000-20,000
Time Frame: 1 month

2 COMPLEXITY OF JOB

EXAMPLE
What We Know:
- 16-page, 4/1 booklet, 8 color photos
- Instructional copy to be written
- Line illustrations of furniture will include exploded views
- Client has photographs
- Illustrations to be subcontracted
- Time needed ....5 hrs

**Total Time
Required**...........................**5 hrs**

YOUR HOURS
What You Know:
-
-
-
-
-
- Time needed ...._____hrs

**Total Time
Required**.............._____**hrs**

3 INITIAL CLIENT MEETING

EXAMPLE
What We Know:
- Client has existing instructional books
- Client has info necessary to write copy
- Time needed ....2 hrs

What We Need:
- Competitors' instructional booklets
- Stats of company logo
- Time needed ....2 hrs

**Total Time
Required** ....**4 hrs**

YOUR HOURS
What You Know:
-
-
- Time needed ...._____hrs

What You Need:
-
-
- Time needed ...._____hrs

**Total Time
Required**................._____**hrs**

4 CONCEPT DEVELOPMENT

EXAMPLE
What We Know:
- Present rough sketches of illustrations
- Client wants 3 layout designs
- Revision time required after final selection
- Time needed ....15 hrs

What We Need:
- Paper samples and dummies
- Time needed ....2 hrs

**Total Time
Required**...........................**17 hrs**

YOUR HOURS
What You Know:
-
-
-
- Time needed ...._____hrs

What You Need:
-
- Time needed...................._____hrs

**Total Time
Required**................._____**hrs**

5 CLIENT REQUIREMENTS FOR PROJECT

EXAMPLE

YOUR HOURS

What We Know:
- Client willing to pay extra to meet deadline
- Client willing to sacrifice quality for speed
- Illustrator and printer must be willing to work with tight deadline
- Time needed ....23 hrs

What You Know:
-
-
-
- Time needed ...._____hrs

Total Time Required...........................**23 hrs**

Total Time Required ...._____**hrs**

6 PREPARING COMPS

EXAMPLE

YOUR HOURS

What We Know:
- Present final or completed illustrations
- Will present layout roughs
- Revisions may be in a tissue layout
- Present copy revisions for approval
- Time needed ....5 hrs

What You Know:
-
-
-
-
- Time needed ...._____hrs

What We Need:
- Copy from client to do roughs
- Client approval of all revisions
- Time needed ....5 hrs

What You Need:
-
-
- Time needed ...._____hrs

Total Time Required...........................**10 hrs**

Total Time Required ...._____**hrs**

TURN PAGE

8 CLIENT MEETINGS

EXAMPLE

YOUR HOURS

What We Know:
- Layout approval
- Copy, illustrations and revisions approval
- Mechanical approval
- Blueline approval
- Time needed ....6 hrs

What You Know:
-
-
-
-
- Time needed ...._____hrs

What We Need:
- Approval/change form for client signature
- Time needed ....1 hr

What You Need:
-
- Time needed ...._____hrs

Total Time Required...........................**7 hrs**

Total Time Required................._____**hrs**

7 MECHANICAL PREPARATION

EXAMPLE

YOUR HOURS

What We Know:
- Okay to show revisions in rough layout
- Typeset copy; prepare and proof boards
- Prepare photos for scanning
- Stat illustrations
- Time needed ....52 hrs

What You Know:
-
-
-
-
- Time needed ...._____hrs

What We Need:
- Review mechanicals with printer
- Get chromalin proofs for client approval
- Request bids (prices/schedules) from vendors/subcontractors
- Time needed ....7 hrs

What You Need:
-
-
- Time needed ...._____hrs

Total Time Required ......**59 hrs**

Total Time Required..._____**hrs**

WORKSHEET 10 CONTINUED

9 CLERICAL/ADMINISTRATIVE WORK

EXAMPLE

What We Know:
• Prepare price estimate and schedule
• Set up billing account
• Time needed ....3 hrs

What We Need:
• Bid confirmation from vendors/subcontractors
• Time needed ....1 hr

Total Time
Required ....4 hrs

YOUR HOURS

What You Know:
•

•

• Time needed..............._____hrs

What You Need:
•

• Time needed..............._____hrs

Total Time
Required ...._____hrs

10 TOTAL PROJECT HOURS

EXAMPLE
• Total Boxes 1-9 to estimate Total Project Hours...129 hrs
(If you charge different rates for activities, divide the box into sections, one section per rate. For example, if you have the same rate for Comp and for Mechanical Prep, assign one section of the box for those total hours.)

YOUR HOURS
•

12 TIME COSTS

EXAMPLE
• Multiply the total number of project hours in Box 11 by your Hourly Fee Rate to get the Total Project Time Costs.........$9,660
(To simplify the example, an average hourly fee of $60 was used. If you charge different rates for activities, multiply the hours for all activities for which you charge the same rate by that rate. Total all the charges. For example, Concept Development + Client Meetings = 70 hrs x $85/hr = $5,950)

YOUR COSTS
•

11 HIDDEN SURPRISE FACTOR

EXAMPLE
• Multiply the amount in Box 10 by .25 (25%); add that to your total project hours to guard against hidden surprises (accidents, emergencies, problems caused by the client, etc.) ....129 + 32 = 161 hrs
(Build a margin into your estimate to avoid cost overruns that anger clients or cost you money. The hidden surprise factor used here is 25% because many snags can occur when a project is being rushed; it's also a good idea to go to this level on a project you've never done before. A 5% security blanket may be enough in many cases.)

YOUR HOURS
•

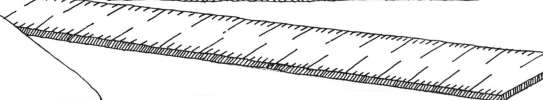

13 URGENCY OF JOB

EXAMPLE

What We Know:

- Short deadline must be met
- Time needed ....35 hrs
- Rush charge.................................$1,050

**Total Time Required/Total
Rush Costs ....35 hrs/$1,050**

- (For a rush project, add your usual charge for overtime or percentage for rush work. For example, 10 hrs of overtime would be $30/hr more (time and a half), so you add $300 to Box 12. An example of a percentage charge is 20 hrs x $60/hr (your hourly fee) = $1200 + (1200 x .05 (5%)) = $1,260.)

YOUR COSTS

What You Know:

-
- Time needed ...._____hrs
- Rush charge ....$_____

**Total Time Required/Total
Rush Costs...._____hrs/$_____**

-

16 TOTAL PROJECT COSTS

EXAMPLE

What We Know:

- Total Project Costs $19,667
- Design used only for booklet, we retain originals ....$0 usage fee

Total Costs $19,667

- (The more rights a client requests, the higher the fee you should charge. Be very careful if a client asks for "all rights" or a "buyout." The fee for the rights involved, if more than one-time rights, must be negotiated with the client and varies from project to project.)

- Sales Tax
  (Calculate sales tax only for the final invoice since it has to be figured on actual costs.)

YOUR COSTS

What You Know:

-
-

Total Costs.................$_____

-

-

14 PRODUCTION COSTS

EXAMPLE

What We Know:

- Typesetting $800
- Printing...3,500
- Separations......................................780
- Illustrations...................................1,550
- Stats..250
- Supplies...200
- Subtotal $7,080
- Markup (15%) 1,062
  (Not all artists charge markup; be consistent in your practice.)
- Total Known Costs........................$8,142

What We Need:

- 10% margin for extra costs..............$815

**Total Production
Costs $8,957**

YOUR COSTS

What You Know:

-
-
-
-
-
-
-
-

- Total Known Costs...............$_____

What You Need:

-

**Total Production
Costs.........................$_____**

15 PRODUCTION AND FEE COSTS

EXAMPLE

- Total the dollar amounts in Boxes 12, 13 and 14 to get the total amount of service fees and production costs........$19,667

YOUR COSTS

-

WORKSHEET 11
PROMOTIONAL MATERIALS

This worksheet shows how to price an uncomplicated media kit for a non-profit organization. Some design firms charge lower rates for nonprofits, but it's more prudent to be consistent in your pricing.

Accurately estimating the cost of any project involves figuring out the cost of the materials and services you'll purchase on behalf of the client as well as the cost of your time. To arrive at an estimate for a job, fill in the amounts requested as you move through the game-board. Skip boxes that do not apply, but otherwise go in order until you reach the goal. Inside each box you'll find an example printed on the left and blank spaces on the right for you to use.

START

1 PROJECT TITLE— PROMOTIONAL FOLDER, MEDIA KIT

Client Name: World Peace Organization
Client Budget: $5,000-10,000
Time Frame: 1 month

2 COMPLEXITY OF JOB

EXAMPLE
What We Know:
- 2-color press/media kit, folder, 3 info sheets, business card
- No halftones or illustrations
- Copy needed
- Research of current trends in media kits
- Preliminary research of organization
- Time needed ....9 hrs

Total Time
Required..............................9 hrs

YOUR HOURS
What You Know:
-
-
-
-
- Time needed ...._____hrs

Total Time
Required................._____hrs

4 CONCEPT DEVELOPMENT

EXAMPLE
What We Know:
- Client wants 3-5 rough layouts
- Revision time needed following final selection
- Select and supervise copywriter
- Time needed ....14 hrs

What We Need:
- Paper sample dummies
- Estimate of mailing costs
- Time needed ....5 hrs

Total Time
Required..............................19 hrs

YOUR HOURS
What You Know:
-
-
-
- Time needed ...._____hrs

What You Need:
-
-
- Time needed....................._____hrs

Total Time
Required................._____hrs

3 INITIAL CLIENT MEETING

EXAMPLE
What We Know:
- Review copy requirements
- Discuss current trends in media kits
- Time needed ....2 hrs

What We Need:
- Client samples of kits preferred
- Time needed ....3 hrs

Total Time
Required..............................5 hrs

YOUR HOURS
What You Know:
-
-
- Time needed ...._____hrs

What You Need:
-
- Time needed ...._____hrs

Total Time
Required................._____hrs

5 CLIENT REQUIREMENTS FOR PROJECT

EXAMPLE

What We Know:
- Deadline is tight
- Must stay under budget and maintain highest possible quality
- Time needed ....3 hrs

Total Time Required............................3 hrs

YOUR HOURS

What You Know:
-
-
- Time needed ...._____hrs

Total Time Required ...._____hrs

6 PREPARING COMPS

EXAMPLE

What We Know:
- Computer-generated comp
- Paper sample dummies
- Copy for review and approval
- Time needed ....10 hrs

What We Need:
- Revision time for comp and copy
- Time needed ....10 hrs

Total Time Required............................20 hrs

YOUR HOURS

What You Know:
-
-
-
- Time needed ...._____hrs

What You Need:
-
- Time needed ...._____hrs

Total Time Required..............._____hrs

TURN PAGE

8 CLIENT MEETINGS

EXAMPLE

What We Know:
- Layout approval
- Comp and copy approval
- Mechanical approval
- Blueline and revisions approval
- Time needed ....6 hrs

What We Need:
- Approval/change forms for client signature
- Time needed ....1 hr

Total Time Required............................7 hrs

YOUR HOURS

What You Know:
-
-
-
-
- Time needed ...._____hrs

What You Need:
-
- Time needed ...._____hrs

Total Time Required..................._____hrs

7 MECHANICAL PREPARATION

EXAMPLE

What We Know:
- Typeset approved copy
- Prepare and proof boards
- Color overlay for second color
- Time needed ....9 hrs

What We Need:
- Request bids (prices/schedules) from vendors/subcontractors
- Time needed ....4 hrs

Total Time Required.........................13 hrs

YOUR HOURS

What You Know:
-
-
-
- Time needed..................._____hrs

What You Need:
-
- Time needed..................._____hrs

Total Time Required ...._____hrs

WORKSHEET 11 *CONTINUED*

9 CLERICAL/ADMINISTRATIVE WORK

EXAMPLE

What We Know:
- Price estimate and schedule prep
- Billing
- Time needed ....2 hrs

What We Need:
- Bid confirmation from vendors/subcontractors
- Time needed ....1 hr

**Total Time
Required**..............................3 hrs

YOUR HOURS

What You Know:
-
-
- Time needed................_____hrs

What You Need:
-
- Time needed................_____hrs

**Total Time
Required** ...._____hrs

10 TOTAL PROJECT HOURS

EXAMPLE
- Total Boxes 1-9 to estimate Total Project Hours...79 hrs
(If you charge different rates for activities, divide the box into sections, one section per rate. For example, if you have the same rate for Comp and for Mechanical Prep, assign one section of the box for those total hours.)

YOUR HOURS
-

12 TIME COSTS

EXAMPLE
- Multiply the total number of project hours in Box 11 by your Hourly Fee Rate to get the Total Project Time Costs $4,980
(To simplify the example, an average hourly fee of $60 was used. If you charge different rates for activities, multiply the hours for all activities for which you charge the same rate by that rate. Total all the charges. For example, Concept Development + Client Meetings = 70 hrs x $85/hr = $5,950)

YOUR COSTS
-

11 HIDDEN SURPRISE FACTOR

EXAMPLE
- Multiply the amount in Box 10 by .05 (5%); add that to Box 10 to guard against hidden surprises (accidents, emergencies, problems caused by the client, etc.).....................79 + 4 = 83 hrs
(Build a margin into your estimate to avoid cost overruns that anger clients or cost you money. Only 5% is used as the hidden surprise factor here, because this client is easy to work with and the project is straightforward.)

YOUR HOURS
-

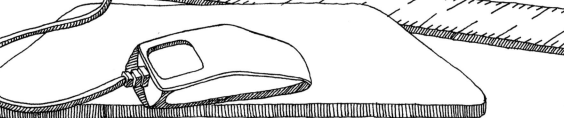

13 URGENCY OF JOB

EXAMPLE
What We Know:
- Deadline is tight; overtime needed
- Time needed ...._____
- Rush charge 10%

**Total Time Required/Total
Rush Costs** ...._____/$498
- (For a rush project, add your overtime charge or percentage for rush work. Enter here only the cost of the extra charge. For example, at $60, time-and-a-half would cost an extra $30/hour. For 3 hours of overtime, the charge would be $90. If the Total Project Time Cost was $1,200 and your rush charge percentage was 20%, a rush charge on the job would be $240 ($1,200 x .2))

YOUR COSTS
What You Know:
-
- Time needed ...._____hrs
- Rush charge......................_____%

**Total Time Required/Total
Rush Costs**...._____hrs/$_____
-

16 TOTAL PROJECT COSTS

EXAMPLE
What We Know:
- Total Project Costs...................$7,047
- One-time usage, we retain originals ....$0 usage fee

Total Costs....................$7,047
- (The more rights a client requests, the higher the fee you should charge. Be very careful if a client asks for "all rights" or a "buyout." The fee for the rights involved, if more than one-time rights, must be negotiated with the client and varies from project to project.)
- Sales Tax
  (Calculate sales tax only for the final invoice since it has to be figured on actual costs.)

YOUR COSTS
What You Know:
-
-

Total Costs.................$_____
-

14 PRODUCTION COSTS

EXAMPLE
What We Know:
- Typesetting $350
- Printing..750
- Stats...60
- Supplies...80
- Subtotal $1,240
- Markup (15%) 186
  (Not all artists charge markup; whether you do or don't, be consistent in your practice.)
- Total Known Costs........................$1,426

What We Need:
- 10% margin for extra costs..............$143

**Total Production
Costs** $1,569

YOUR COSTS
What You Know:
-
-
-
-
-
-

- Total Known Costs..............$_____

What You Need:
-

**Total Production
Costs**........................$_____

15 PRODUCTION AND FEE COSTS

EXAMPLE
- Add the dollar amounts in Boxes 12, 13 and 14 to get the total amount of service fees and production costs.............$7,047

YOUR COSTS
-

WORKSHEET 12

CATALOG

This example demonstrates how to price a multipage catalog. This type of project is easier to produce if it is computer-generated. Otherwise, hand-drawn tissue layouts, typesetting and paste-up for so many pages make this project time-consuming and frustrating.

Accurately estimating the cost of any project involves figuring out the cost of the materials and services you'll purchase on behalf of the client as well as the cost of your time. To arrive at an estimate for a job, fill in the amounts requested as you move through the game-board. Skip boxes that do not apply, but otherwise go in order until you reach the goal. In each box, you'll find an example printed on the left and blank spaces on the right for you to use.

START

1 PROJECT TITLE— PRODUCT CATALOG

Client Name: Johnston Tool & Die Company
Client Budget: $45,000-50,000
Time Frame: 5 months

2 COMPLEXITY OF JOB

EXAMPLE

What We Know:
- 256-page, 3-color industrial product catalog, 250 b&w photos
- Airbrushed photos
- Computer-generated layout, type and mechanicals
- Contract must clearly state kill fee
- Press check to be done
- Time needed ....5 hrs

Total Time
Required..............................5 hrs

YOUR HOURS

What You Know:
- •
- •
- •
- •
- •
- Time needed ...._____hrs

Total Time
Required..............._____hrs

4 CONCEPT DEVELOPMENT

EXAMPLE

What We Know:
- Client wants 3-5 cover layouts plus page grids
- Revision time needed following final selection
- Time needed ....20 hrs

What We Need:
- Select industrial photographer & airbrush artist
- Time needed ....7 hrs

Total Time
Required...........................27 hrs

YOUR HOURS

What You Know:
- •
- •
- Time needed ...._____hrs

What You Need:
- •
- Time needed...................._____hrs

Total Time
Required................._____hrs

3 INITIAL CLIENT MEETING

EXAMPLE

What We Know:
- Review old catalogs, prepare recommendations
- Show samples of computer-generated catalogs
- Time needed ....3 hrs

What We Need:
- Client-generated copy
- Competitors' catalogs
- Time needed ....5 hrs

Total Time
Required...........................8 hrs

YOUR HOURS

What You Know:
- •
- •
- Time needed ...._____hrs

What You Need:
- •
- •
- Time needed ...._____hrs

Total Time
Required................._____hrs

5 CLIENT REQUIREMENTS FOR PROJECT

EXAMPLE

What We Know:
- High-quality product photos & airbrushing
- Clean, simple, page layouts
- 3 colors to highlight specs and frame photos
- We supervise photo shoot and airbrushing
- Time needed ....55 hrs

Total Time Required..........................**55 hrs**

YOUR HOURS

What You Know:
-
-
-
-
- Time needed ...._____hrs

Total Time Required ...._____hrs

TURN PAGE

6 PREPARING COMPS

EXAMPLE

What We Know:
- Don't need fully developed comps
- Must revise cover selection and page grid
- Input copy for type
- Show client cover and pages with type
- Time needed ....95 hrs

What We Need:
- Final copy
- Paper samples
- Art direct photo shoot
- Send out photos for airbrushing
- Time needed ....30 hrs

Total Time Required..........................**125 hrs**

YOUR HOURS

What You Know:
-
-
-
-
- Time needed....................._____hrs

What You Need:
-
-
-
-
- Time needed....................._____hrs

Total Time Required..............._____hrs

8 CLIENT MEETINGS

EXAMPLE

What We Know:
- Layout and comp approvals
- Photography/airbrushing approval
- Mechanical & blueline approval
- Time needed ....17 hrs

What We Need:
- Approval/change form for client signature
- Limits on rounds of revisions
- Time needed ....1 hr

Total Time Required..........................**18 hrs**

YOUR HOURS

What You Know:
-
-
-
- Time needed ...._____hrs

What You Need:
-
-
- Time needed ...._____hrs

Total Time Required.................._____hrs

7 MECHANICAL PREPARATION

EXAMPLE

What We Know:
- Generate electronic keylines
- Final revisions due for copy
- Make all final type changes
- Photos scan for position prints
- Reproduce photos as halftones
- Time needed ....52 hrs

What We Need:
- Request bids (prices/schedules) from vendors/subcontractors
- Time needed ....13 hrs

Total Time Required ....**65 hrs**

YOUR HOURS

What You Know:
-
-
-
-
-
- Time needed..................._____hrs

What You Need:
-
- Time needed..................._____hrs

Total Time Required.................._____hrs

WORKSHEET 12 *CONTINUED*

9 CLERICAL/ADMINISTRATIVE WORK

EXAMPLE

What We Know:
- Prepare price estimate and schedule
- Set up billing account
- Time needed ....3 hrs

What We Need:
- Bid confirmation from vendors/subcontractors
- Time needed ....1 hr

Total Time
Required ....4 hrs

YOUR HOURS

What You Know:
-
-
- Time needed..............._____hrs

What You Need:
-
- Time needed..............._____hrs

Total Time
Required ...._____hrs

10 TOTAL PROJECT HOURS

EXAMPLE
- Total Boxes 1-9 to estimate Total Project Hours..307 hrs
  (If you charge different rates for activities, divide the box into sections, one section per rate. For example, if you have the same rate for Comp and for Mechanical Prep, assign one section of the box for those total hours.)

YOUR HOURS
-

12 TIME COSTS

EXAMPLE
- Multiply the total number of project hours in Box 11 by your Hourly Fee Rate to get the Total Project Time Costs.......$21,180
  (To simplify the example, an average hourly fee of $60 has been used. If you charge different rates for activities, multiply the hours for all activities for which you charge the same rate by that rate. Total all the charges. For example, Concept Development + Client Meetings = 70 hrs x $85/hr = $5,950)

YOUR COSTS
-

11 HIDDEN SURPRISE FACTOR

EXAMPLE
- Multiply the amount in Box 10 by .15 (15%); add that to Box 10 to guard against hidden surprises (accidents, emergencies, problems caused by the client, etc.).................307 + 46 = 353 hrs
  (Build a margin into your estimate to avoid cost overruns that anger clients or cost you money. The hidden surprise factor used here is 15% because the project is complex; it's also a good idea to go to this level on a project you've never done before. A 5% security blanket may be enough in many cases.)

YOUR HOURS
-

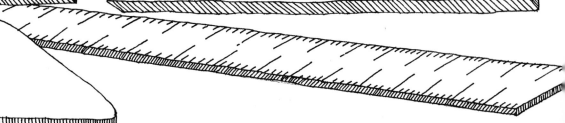

13 URGENCY OF JOB

EXAMPLE

What We Know:
- Deadline is manageable; no overtime
- Time needed ....0 hrs
- Rush charge.................................0%/$0

Total Time Required/Total Rush Costs ....0 hrs/$0
- (For a rush project, add your overtime charge or percentage for rush work. Enter here only the cost of the extra charge. For example, at $60, time-and-a-half would cost an extra $30/hour. For 3 hours of overtime, the charge would be $90. If the Total Project Time Cost was $1,200 and your rush charge percentage was 20%, a rush charge on the job would be $240 ($1,200 x .2))

YOUR COSTS

What You Know:
-
- Time needed ...._____hrs
- Rush charge............_____%/$_____

Total Time Required/Total Rush Costs...._____hrs/$_____
-

14 PRODUCTION COSTS

EXAMPLE

What We Know:
- Computer usage................................$450
- Printing..7,500
- Photography....................................8,750
- Airbrushing......................................2,500
- Halftones...1,100
- Supplies...250
- Subtotal.......................................$20,550
- Markup (20%)................................4,110
  (Not all artists charge markup; whether you do or don't, be consistent in your practice.)
- Total Known Costs $24,660

What We Need:
- 10% margin for extra costs...........$2,466

Total Production Costs $27,126

YOUR COSTS

What You Know:
-
-
-
-
-
-
-
-
-
- Total Known Costs..............$_____

What You Need:
-

Total Production Costs.........................$_____

16 TOTAL PROJECT COSTS

EXAMPLE

What We Know:
- Total Project Costs....................$48,306
- One time use only, we retain originals ....$0 usage fee

Total Costs $48,306
- (The more rights a client requests, the higher the fee you should charge. Be very careful if a client asks for "all rights" or a "buyout." The fee for the rights involved, if more than one-time rights, must be negotiated with the client and varies from project to project.)
- Sales Tax
  (Calculate sales tax only for the final invoice since it has to be figured on actual costs.)

YOUR COSTS

What You Know:
-
-

Total Costs.................$_____
-

15 PRODUCTION AND FEE COSTS

EXAMPLE
- Add the dollar amounts in Boxes 12, 13 and 14 to get the total amount of service fees and production costs...........$48,306

YOUR COSTS
-

WORKSHEET 13
ANNUAL REPORT

An annual report is one of the more complex projects designers handle. Since most of them involve presentations, do not underestimate the time involved in the preparation. As with all presentations or preliminary work, prep time should always be figured in the price.

Accurately estimating the cost of any project involves figuring out the cost of the materials and services you'll purchase on behalf of the client as well as the cost of your time. To arrive at an estimate for a job, fill in the amounts requested as you move through the gameboard. Skip boxes that do not apply, but otherwise go in order until you reach the goal. Inside each box, you'll find an example printed on the left and blank spaces on the right for you to use.

START

1 PROJECT TITLE— CORPORATE ANNUAL REPORT

Client Name: Community Bank
Client Budget: $40,000-45,000
Time Frame: 9 months

2 COMPLEXITY OF JOB

EXAMPLE

What We Know:
- 36-page annual report, 4-color, ⅔ editorial, ⅓ financial
- Photos plus illustrations
- We write copy
- We generate charts and graphs
- Client difficult to please, expected to make last-minute changes
- All phases to be approved by bank officers and p.r. director
- Time needed ....4 hrs

**Total Time
Required..........................4 hrs**

YOUR HOURS

What You Know:
-
-
-
-
-
- Time needed ...._____hrs

**Total Time
Required ...._____hrs**

4 CONCEPT DEVELOPMENT

EXAMPLE

What We Know:
- Prep for presentation
- 3 comps of covers, page layouts
- Written proposal of strategy, budget and schedule
- Time needed ....40 hrs

What We Need:
- Samples from 3 photographers
- Copies of proposal for participants
- Time needed ....5 hrs

**Total Time
Required..........................45 hrs**

YOUR HOURS

What You Know:
-
-
-
- Time needed ...._____hrs

What You Need:
-
-
- Time needed...................._____hrs

**Total Time
Required.................._____hrs**

3 INITIAL CLIENT MEETING

EXAMPLE

What We Know:
- Discuss market demographics and desired impact of report
- Review bank history for inclusion
- Time needed ....3 hrs

What We Need:
- Competitive annual reports
- Client's past reports
- Time needed ....2 hrs

**Total Time
Required..........................5 hrs**

YOUR HOURS

What You Know:
-
-
- Time needed ...._____hrs

What You Need:
-
-
- Time needed ...._____hrs

**Total Time
Required................._____hrs**

5 CLIENT REQUIREMENTS FOR PROJECT

EXAMPLE

What We Know:
- High-quality piece
- Historical theme
- Wants involvement in all phases
- Time needed ....10 hrs

**Total Time
Required**...........................**10 hrs**

YOUR HOURS

What You Know:
-
-
-
- Time needed ...._____hrs

**Total Time
Required** ...._____**hrs**

6 PREPARING COMPS

EXAMPLE

What We Know:
- Plan time for revising selected design
- Layout spreads for all pages
- Interview bank personnel
- Supervise copywriter
- Art direct photo shoot & illustrations
- Time needed ....150 hrs

What We Need:
- Edit chromes
- Arrange copy revisions
- Paper sample dummies
- Time needed ....20 hrs

**Total Time
Required**..........................**170 hrs**

YOUR HOURS

What You Know:
-
-
-
-
-
- Time needed................._____hrs

What You Need:
-
-
-
- Time needed................._____hrs

**Total Time
Required** ...._____**hrs**

TURN PAGE

8 CLIENT MEETINGS

EXAMPLE

What We Know:
- Concept presentation
- Layout and copy revision approval
- Photo/chrome selection approval
- Mechanical approval
- Time needed ....20 hrs

What We Need:
- Approval/change form for client signature
- Time needed ....1 hr

Total Time Required ....**21 hrs**

YOUR HOURS

What You Know:
-
-
-
-
- Time needed ...._____hrs

What You Need:
-
- Time needed ...._____hrs

Total Time Required ..._____**hrs**

7 MECHANICAL PREPARATION

EXAMPLE

What We Know:
- Typesetting
- Prepare/proof boards for 16-page spreads & cover spreads
- Cut overlays, paste-up type, put down position stats
- Prepare photos for scanning
- Time needed ....45 hrs

What We Need:
- Request bids (prices/schedules) from vendors/subcontractors
- Time needed ....4 hrs

**Total Time
Required** ....**49 hrs**

YOUR HOURS

What You Know:
-
-
-
- Time needed................._____hrs

What You Need:
-
- Time needed................._____hrs

**Total Time
Required** ...._____**hrs**

9 CLERICAL/ADMINISTRATIVE WORK

EXAMPLE

What We Know:
- Prepare price estimate and schedule
- Set up billing account
- Time needed ....3 hrs

What We Need:
- Bid confirmation from vendors/subcontractors
- Time needed ....1 hr

Total Time Required.............................4 hrs

YOUR HOURS

What You Know:
-
-
- Time needed..............._____hrs

What You Need:
-
- Time needed..............._____hrs

Total Time Required............_____hrs

10 TOTAL PROJECT HOURS

EXAMPLE
- Total Boxes 1-9 to estimate Total Project Hours..308 hrs
(If you charge different rates for activities, divide the box into sections, one section per rate. For example, if you have the same rate for Comp and for Mechanical Prep, assign one section of the box for those total hours.)

YOUR HOURS
-

12 TIME COSTS

EXAMPLE
- Multiply the total number of project hours in Box 11 by your Hourly Fee Rate to get the Total Project Time Costs.......$22,200
(To simplify the example, an average hourly fee of $60 was used. If you charge different rates for activities, multiply the hours for all activities for which you charge the same rate by that rate. Total all the charges. For example, Concept Development + Client Meetings = 70 hrs x $85/hr = $5,950)

YOUR COSTS
-

11 HIDDEN SURPRISE FACTOR

EXAMPLE
- Multiply the amount in Box 10 by .20 (20%); add that to Box 10 to guard against hidden surprises (accidents, emergencies, problems caused by the client, etc.)................308 + 61 = 369 hrs
(Build a margin into your estimate to avoid cost overruns that anger clients or cost you money. The hidden surprise factor used is 20% because this client is difficult to work with. It's a good idea to go to 15% on a project you've never done before, but a 5% security blanket may be enough in many cases.)

YOUR HOURS
-

13 URGENCY OF JOB

EXAMPLE
What We Know:
- Deadline is manageable; no overtime
- Time needed ....0 hrs
- Rush charge ....0%/$0

Total Time Required/Total Rush Costs ....0 hrs/$0
- (For a rush project, add your overtime charge or percentage for rush work. Enter here only the cost of the extra charge. For example, at $60, time-and-a-half would cost an extra $30/hour. For 3 hours of overtime, the charge would be $90. If the Total Project Time Cost was $1,200 and your rush charge percentage was 20%, a rush charge on the job would be $240 ($1,200 x .2))

YOUR COSTS
What You Know:
-
- Time needed ...._____hrs
- Rush charge............._____%/$_____

Total Time Required/Total Rush Costs...._____hrs/$_____
-

16 TOTAL PROJECT COSTS

EXAMPLE
What We Know:
- Total Project Costs.....................$44,528
- One-time use, we retain originals..............................$0 usage fee

Total Costs $44,528
- (The more rights a client requests, the higher the fee you should charge. Be very careful if a client asks for "all rights" or a "buyout." The fee for the rights involved, if more than one-time rights, must be negotiated with the client and varies from project to project.)
- Sales Tax
  (Calculate sales tax only for the final invoice since it has to be figured on actual costs.)

YOUR COSTS
What You Know:
-
-

Total Costs.................$_____
-

14 PRODUCTION COSTS

EXAMPLE
What We Know:
- Typesetting ....$ 2,200
- Printing...10,500
- Photography 2,550
- Illustrations...800
- Stats...250
- Supplies..150
- Color separations............................1,200
- Subtotal $17,650
- Markup (15%) 2,648
  (Not all artists charge markup; whether you do or don't, be consistent in your practice.)
- Total Known Costs $20,298

What We Need:
- 10% margin for extra costs............$2,030

Total Production Costs $22,328

YOUR COSTS
What You Know:
-
-
-
-
-
-
-
-
-
- Total Known Costs.............$ _____

What You Need:
-

Total Production Costs ....$_____

15 PRODUCTION AND FEE COSTS

EXAMPLE
- Add the dollar amounts in Boxes 12, 13 and 14 to get the total amount of service fees and production costs $44,528

YOUR COSTS
-

WORKSHEET 14
BOOK JACKET DESIGN

This example is a book dust jacket design involving type only. Some projects may require both type and illustration, which the designer may do if it is within her range of capabilities. If not, the designer will do a rough sketch of the illustration concept for a freelancer to follow.

Accurately estimating the cost of any project involves figuring out the cost of the materials and services you'll purchase on behalf of the client as well as the cost of your time. To arrive at an estimate for a job, fill in the amounts requested as you move through the gameboard. Skip boxes that do not apply, but otherwise go in order until you reach the goal. Inside each box, you'll find an example printed on the left and blank spaces on the right for you to use.

1 PROJECT TITLE—BOOK DUST JACKET DESIGN

Client Name: Wilson, Peabody & Robare Publishing Co.
Client Budget: $750-900
Time Frame: 2 weeks

2 COMPLEXITY OF JOB

EXAMPLE

What We Know:
- Wrap-around dust jacket for a hardcover trade publication
- Design involves type only
- We supply disk; client transfers to film or high-resolution paper
- Client has clear ideas about what jacket needs to look like
- Contract must clearly state kill fee
- Time needed ....1/2 hr

Total Time Required ....1/2 hr

YOUR HOURS

What You Know:
-
-
-
-
-
- Time needed ...._____hrs

Total Time Required ...._____hrs

4 CONCEPT DEVELOPMENT

EXAMPLE

What We Know:
- Client wants 2-3 computerized roughs
- Time needed ....2 hrs

What We Need:
- Fax roughs to client for approval or changes
- Time needed ....1 hr

Total Time Required ....3 hrs

YOUR HOURS

What You Know:
-
- Time needed ...._____hrs

What You Need:
-
- Time needed..................._____hrs

Total Time Required ...._____hrs

3 INITIAL CLIENT MEETING

EXAMPLE

What We Know:
- Phone meeting—client explains concept, faxes job brief
- Client faxes title and marketing copy
- Time needed ....1/2 hr

What We Need:
- Trim size, spine width and due date
- Time needed...................................0 hrs

Total Time Required ....1/2 hr

YOUR HOURS

What You Know:
-
-
- Time needed ...._____hrs

What You Need:
-
- Time needed ...._____hrs

Total Time Required ...._____hrs

5 CLIENT REQUIREMENTS FOR PROJECT

EXAMPLE

What We Know:
- Sophisticated design required
- Fixed budget
- Plan time carefully
- Time needed ....½ hr

**Total Time
Required** ....½ hr

YOUR HOURS

What You Know:
-
-
-
- Time needed ...._____hrs

**Total Time
Required** ...._____hrs

6 PREPARING COMPS

EXAMPLE

What We Know:
- Develop concept at half size from final rough
- Generate color output
- Time needed ....2 hrs

What We Need:
- Send color copy of tight comp to client overnight
- Time needed....................................½ hr

**Total Time
Required** ....2½ hrs

YOUR HOURS

What You Know:
-
-
- Time needed ...._____hrs

What You Need:
-
- Time needed ...._____hrs

**Total Time
Required** ...._____hrs

TURN PAGE

8 CLIENT MEETINGS

EXAMPLE

What We Know:
- Initial approval of roughs via phone/fax
- Approval of tight comp via mail/phone
- Approval of electronic keyline and disk via mail/phone
- Time needed ....1 hr

What We Need:
- Approval/change forms for client signature
- Time needed....................................½ hr

**Total Time
Required** ....1½ hrs

YOUR HOURS

What You Know:
-
-
-
- Time needed ...._____hrs

What You Need:
-
- Time needed ...._____hrs

**Total Time
Required** ...._____hrs

7 MECHANICAL PREPARATION

EXAMPLE

What We Know:
- No mechanical needed
- Client to fax changes on comp
- Produce electronic keyline of final design to size
- Proof
- Send disk out to service bureau for color output
- Time needed ....3 hrs

What We Need:
- Overnight color copy and disk to client
- Time needed..............................½ hr

**Total Time
Required** ....3½ hrs

YOUR HOURS

What You Know:
-
-
-
-
-
- Time needed ...._____hrs

What You Need:
-
- Time needed ...._____hrs

**Total Time
Required** ...._____hrs

WORKSHEET 14 CONTINUED

9 CLERICAL/ADMINISTRATIVE WORK

EXAMPLE

What We Know:
- Prepare price estimate and schedule
- Set up billing account
- Time needed......................................½ hr

What We Need:
- Contract
- Time needed......................................½ hr

Total Time
Required ....1 hr

YOUR HOURS

What You Know:
-
-
- Time needed..............._____hrs

What You Need:
-
- Time needed..............._____hrs

Total Time
Required ...._____hrs

12 TIME COSTS

EXAMPLE
- Multiply the total number of project hours in Box 11 by your Hourly Fee Rate to get the Total Project Time Costs............$840 (To simplify the example, an average hourly fee of $60 was used. If you charge different rates for activities, multiply the hours for all activities for which you charge the same rate by that rate. Total all the charges. For example, Concept Development + Client Meetings = 70 hrs x $85/hr = $5,950)

YOUR COSTS
-

10 TOTAL PROJECT HOURS

EXAMPLE
- Add your hours in Boxes 1-9 to estimate the Total Project Hours ....13 hrs (If you charge different rates for activities, divide the box into sections, one section per rate. For example, if you have the same rate for Comp and for Mechanical Prep, assign one section of the box for those total hours.)

YOUR HOURS
-

11 HIDDEN SURPRISE FACTOR

EXAMPLE
- Multiply the amount in Box 10 by .05 (5%); add that to Box 10 to guard against hidden surprises (accidents, emergencies, problems caused by the client, etc.)....................13 + 1 = 14 hrs (Build a margin into your estimate to avoid cost overruns that anger clients or cost you money. The hidden surprise factor used here is 5% because this project is fairly simple and straightforward. It's a good idea to go to 15% on a project you've never done before, but a 5% security blanket may be enough in many cases.)

YOUR HOURS
-

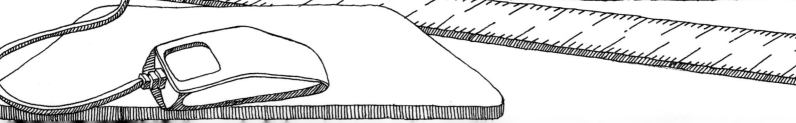

13 URGENCY OF JOB

EXAMPLE
What We Know:
- Deadline is manageable; no overtime
- Time needed ....0 hrs
- Rush charge ....0%/$0

**Total Time Required/Total
Rush Costs ....0 hrs/$0**
- (For a rush project, add your overtime charge or percentage for rush work. Enter here only the cost of the extra charge. For example, at $60, time-and-a-half would cost an extra $30/hour. For 3 hours of overtime, the charge would be $90. If the Total Project Time Cost was $1,200 and your rush charge percentage was 20%, a rush charge on the job would be $240 ($1,200 x .2))

YOUR COSTS
What You Know:
-
- Time needed ...._____hrs
- Rush charge............_____%/$_____

**Total Time Required/Total
Rush Costs...._____hrs/$_____**
-

14 PRODUCTION COSTS

EXAMPLE
What We Know:
- Service bureau color copy.................$10
- Supplies..5
- Mailing/fax costs 25
- Subtotal $40
- Markup (20%) 8
  (Not all artists charge markup; whether you do or don't, be consistent in your practice.)
- Total Known Costs.............................$48

What We Need:
- 10% margin for extra costs $5

**Total Production
Costs $53**

YOUR COSTS
What You Know:
-
-
-
-
-
- Total Known Costs...............$_____

What You Need:
-

**Total Production
Costs.........................$_____**

16 TOTAL PROJECT COSTS

EXAMPLE
What We Know:
- Total Project Costs..........................$893
- Fee includes all rights ....$0 usage fee

Total Costs $893
- (The more rights a client requests, the higher the fee you should charge. Be very careful if a client asks for "all rights" or a "buyout." The fee for the rights involved, if more than one-time rights, must be negotiated with the client and varies from project to project.)
- Sales Tax
  (Calculate sales tax only for the final invoice since it has to be figured on actual costs.)

YOUR COSTS
What You Know:
-
-

Total Costs.................$_____
-

-

15 PRODUCTION AND FEE COSTS

EXAMPLE
- Total the dollar amounts in Boxes 12, 13 and 14 to get the total amount of service fees and production costs $893

YOUR COSTS
-

WORKSHEET 15
NEWSLETTER/PUBLICATION DESIGN

This is an example of a newsletter design that does not involve production. Many clients prefer to buy a newsletter design/grid that can be used for in-house production. In this case, the disk and all rights must be sold.

Accurately estimating the cost of any project involves figuring out the cost of the materials and services you'll purchase on behalf of the client as well as the cost of your time. To arrive at an estimate for a job, fill in the amounts requested as you move through the gameboard. Skip boxes that do not apply, but otherwise go in order until you reach the goal. Inside each box, you'll find an example printed on the left and blank spaces on the right for you to use.

START

1 PROJECT TITLE— STOCKHOLDERS' NEWSLETTER

Client Name: MGC Computer Corporation
Client Budget: $3,500-4,500
Time Frame: 2 weeks

2 COMPLEXITY OF JOB

EXAMPLE
What We Know:
- 8-page, 2-color, computer-generated design, masthead and page layout grid
- Clean, simple design
- Nameplate exists
- Time needed ....2 hrs

Total Time
Required.............................2 hrs

YOUR HOURS
What You Know:
-
-
-
- Time needed................_____hrs

Total Time
Required................._____hrs

4 CONCEPT DEVELOPMENT

EXAMPLE
What We Know:
- Client wants 3 cover/masthead designs and page layouts
- Revision time needed following final selection
- Time needed ....15 hrs

What We Need:
- Laser color copies to indicate second color options and use
- Scanned sample photos
- Time needed ....3 hrs

Total Time
Required...........................18 hrs

YOUR HOURS
What You Know:
-
-
- Time needed ...._____hrs

What You Need:
-
-
- Time needed....................._____hrs

Total Time
Required.................._____hrs

3 INITIAL CLIENT MEETING

EXAMPLE
What We Know:
- Discuss newsletter audience and content
- Typical number of photos, features and special columns
- Time needed ....1 hr

What We Need:
- Competitive newsletter
- Existing newsletter layouts client likes
- Time needed ....1 hr

Total Time
Required...........................2 hrs

YOUR HOURS
What You Know:
-
-
- Time needed ...._____hrs

What You Need:
-
-
- Time needed....................._____hrs

Total Time
Required.................._____hrs

5 CLIENT REQUIREMENTS FOR PROJECT

TURN PAGE

EXAMPLE

What We Know:
- Deadline tight, overtime will be needed
- Corporate look, not glitzy
- Flexible layout grid
- Time needed ....1 hr

**Total Time
Required** ....1 hr

YOUR HOURS

What You Know:
-
-
-
- Time needed ...._____hrs

**Total Time
Required** ...._____hrs

6 PREPARING COMPS

EXAMPLE

What We Know:
- Color comps of final design printed in second color
- Printouts on a variety of paper samples
- Time needed ....5 hrs

What We Need:
- Printing prices for paper samples
- 3 suggested text typefaces
- Extra comps for board of directors meeting
- Time needed. ....5 hrs

**Total Time
Required** ....10 hrs

YOUR HOURS

What You Know:
-
-
- Time needed................._____hrs

What You Need:
-
-
-
- Time needed................._____hrs

**Total Time
Required** ...._____hrs

8 CLIENT MEETINGS

EXAMPLE

What We Know:
- Concept layout approval
- Comp approval
- Final disk approval
- Time needed ....3 hrs

What We Need:
- Approval/change forms for client signature
- Time needed ....1 hr

**Total Time
Required** ....4 hrs

YOUR HOURS

What You Know:
-
-
-
- Time needed ...._____hrs

What You Need:
-
- Time needed ...._____hrs

**Total Time
Required** ...._____hrs

7 MECHANICAL PREPARATION

EXAMPLE

What We Know:
- No mechanicals required
- Client gets two disk copies of cover, masthead and layout designs
- Keylines for second color on disk
- Time needed ....4 hrs

What We Need:
- Laser proofs for client approval
- Time needed ....1 hr

**Total Time
Required** ....5 hrs

YOUR HOURS

What You Know:
-
-
-
- Time needed................._____hrs

What You Need:
-
- Time needed................._____hrs

**Total Time
Required** ...._____hrs

WORKSHEET 15 *CONTINUED*

9 CLERICAL/ADMINISTRATIVE WORK

EXAMPLE

What We Know:
- Prepare price estimate and schedule
- Set up billing account
- Time needed ....2 hrs

Total Time
Required ....2 hrs

YOUR HOURS

What You Know:
-
-
- Time needed ...._____hrs

Total Time
Required ...._____hrs

10 TOTAL PROJECT HOURS

EXAMPLE

- Total Boxes 1-9 to estimate Total Project Hours...44 hrs
(If you charge different rates for activities, divide the box into sections, one section per rate. For example, if you have the same rate for Comp and for Mechanical Prep, assign one section of the box for those total hours.)

YOUR HOURS

-

12 TIME COSTS

EXAMPLE

- Multiply the total number of project hours in Box 11 by your Hourly Fee Rate to get the Total Project Time Costs........$2,760
(To simplify the example, an average hourly fee of $60 has been used. If you charge different rates for activities, multiply the hours for all activities for which you charge the same rate by that rate. Total all the charges. For example, Concept Development + Client Meetings = 70 hrs x $85/hr = $5,950)

YOUR COSTS

-

11 HIDDEN SURPRISE FACTOR

EXAMPLE

- Multiply the amount in Box 10 by .05 (5%); add that to Box 10 to guard against hidden surprises (accidents, emergencies, problems caused by the client, etc.) ....44 + 2 = 46 hrs
(Build a margin into your estimate to avoid cost overruns that anger clients or cost you money. Only 5% is used as the hidden surprise factor here because this client is easy to work with and the project doesn't involve production.)

YOUR HOURS

-

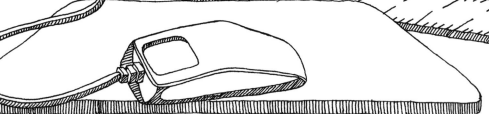

13 URGENCY OF JOB

EXAMPLE

What We Know:
- Deadline is manageable
- Time needed ....5 hrs
- Rush charge $30/hr

**Total Time Required/Total
Rush Costs ....5 hrs/$150.00**
- (For a rush project, add your overtime charge or percentage for rush work. Enter here only the cost of the extra charge. For example, at $60, time-and-a-half would cost an extra $30/hour. For 3 hours of overtime, the charge would be $90. If the Total Project Time Cost was $1,200 and your rush charge percentage was 20%, a rush charge on the job would be $240 ($1,200 x .2))

YOUR COSTS

What You Know:
-
- Time needed ...._____hrs
- Rush charge...................$_____/hr

**Total Time Required/Total
Rush Costs...._____hrs/$_____**
-

16 TOTAL PROJECT COSTS

GOAL

EXAMPLE

What We Know:
- Total Project Costs.......................$3,416
- Client wants all rights ......$500 usage fee

Total Costs $3,916
- (The more rights a client requests, the higher the fee you should charge. Be very careful if a client asks for "all rights" or a "buyout." The fee for the rights involved, if more than one-time rights, must be negotiated with the client and varies from project to project.)
- Sales Tax
  (Calculate sales tax only for the final invoice since it has to be figured on actual costs.)

YOUR COSTS

What You Know:
-
-

Total Costs.................$_____
-

-

14 PRODUCTION COSTS

EXAMPLE

What We Know:
- Computer usage...............................$325
- Supplies...75
- Subtotal $400
- Markup (15%) 60

  (Not all artists charge markup; whether you do or don't, be consistent in your practice.)
- Total Known Costs $460

What We Need:
- 10% margin for extra costs................$46

**Total Production
Costs $506**

YOUR COSTS

What You Know:
-
-
-
-

- Total Known Costs...........$_____

What You Need:
-

**Total Production
Costs ....$_____**

15 PRODUCTION AND FEE COSTS

EXAMPLE
- Add the dollar amounts in Boxes 12, 13 and 14 to get the total amount of service fees and production costs...........$3,416

YOUR COSTS
-

WORKSHEET 16

MAGAZINE COVER REDESIGN

This worksheet involves pricing a cover redesign for a national magazine with moderate circulation. The fee, as with most magazines, is a set page rate including expenses. Figure your time and costs carefully to ensure that this is a profitable job. The client is buying all rights and the disk.

Accurately estimating the cost of any project involves figuring out your time and the cost of materials and services you'll purchase on behalf of the client. To arrive at an estimate for a job, fill in the amounts requested as you move through the gameboard. Skip boxes that do not apply, but otherwise go in order until you reach the goal. Inside each box, you'll find an example printed on the left and blank spaces on the right for you to use.

1 PROJECT TITLE— INVESTMENT MAGAZINE COVER REDESIGN

Client Name: Financial Planning Publications
Client Budget: $2,500
Time Frame: 2 weeks

2 COMPLEXITY OF JOB

EXAMPLE
What We Know:
- Client wants a new, contemporary look; logo stays the same
- We will research competitive publications
- 3-color design, new typeface required
- Time needed ....1 hr

Total Time Required ....1 hr

YOUR HOURS
What You Know:
-
-
-
- Time needed ...._____hrs

Total Time Required..............._____hrs

4 CONCEPT DEVELOPMENT

EXAMPLE
What We Know:
- Client wants 2-3 computer-generated layouts with color indicated
- Fax layouts for client review/approval; send approval/change form
- Time needed ....6 hrs

What We Need:
- Stats of logo
- Revision time
- Time needed ....2 hrs

Total Time Required ....8 hrs

YOUR HOURS
What You Know:
-
-
- Time needed ...._____hrs

What You Need:
-
-
- Time needed ...._____hrs

Total Time Required..............._____hrs

3 INITIAL CLIENT MEETING

EXAMPLE
What We Know:
- Phone meeting to discuss reader demographics, market trends & competitors' covers
- Time needed ....1 hr

What We Need:
- Past covers, competitors' covers & cover specifications
- Contract clearly stating kill and usage fees
- Time needed ....1 hr

Total Time Required ....2 hrs

YOUR HOURS
What You Know:
-
- Time needed ...._____hrs

What You Need:
-
-
- Time needed ...._____hrs

Total Time Required..............._____hrs

5 CLIENT REQUIREMENTS FOR PROJECT

EXAMPLE

What We Know:
- High-end, complex production; build in extra time
- Client prone to indecision
- Time needed ....2 hrs

Total Time Required.............................2 hrs

YOUR HOURS

What You Know:
-
-
- Time needed ...._____hrs

Total Time Required ...._____hrs

TURN PAGE

8 CLIENT MEETINGS

EXAMPLE

What We Know:
- Approval of initial layouts
- Approval of comp
- Review of first two rounds of revisions
- Approval of final output
- Time needed ....2 hrs

What We Need:
- Approval/change forms for client signature
- Time needed ....1 hr

Total Time Required ....3 hrs

YOUR HOURS

What You Know:
-
-
-
-
- Time needed ...._____hrs

What You Need:
-
- Time needed ...._____hrs

Total Time Required................._____hrs

6 PREPARING COMPS

EXAMPLE

What We Know:
- 1 full-color concept comp showing revisions
- Send disk to service bureau for color output
- Time needed ....5 hrs

What We Need:
- Send color copy overnight to client
- Discuss comp/revisions by phone
- Allow time for further revisions
- Time needed ....4 hrs

Total Time Required.............................9 hrs

YOUR HOURS

What You Know:
-
-
- Time needed ...._____hrs

What You Need:
-
-
-
- Time needed ...._____hrs

Total Time Required ...._____hrs

7 MECHANICAL PREPARATION

EXAMPLE

What We Know:
- Additional revisions necessary
- Must produce electronic keyline separations for each color
- Must proof
- Make back-up disk
- Send to service bureau for output
- Time needed ....6 hrs

Total Time Required ....6 hrs

YOUR HOURS

What You Know:
-
-
-
-
- Time needed ...._____hrs

Total Time Required ...._____hrs

WORKSHEET 16 *CONTINUED*

9 CLERICAL/ADMINISTRATIVE WORK

EXAMPLE

What We Know:

• Prepare price estimate and schedule

• Set up billing account

• Time needed ....1 hr

**Total Time
Required** ....1 hr

YOUR HOURS

What You Know:

•

•

• Time needed..............._____hrs

**Total Time
Required** ...._____hrs

10 TOTAL PROJECT HOURS

EXAMPLE

• Add your hours in Boxes 1-9 to estimate the Total Project Hours. ....32 hrs
(If you charge different rates for activities, divide the box into sections, one section per rate. For example, if you have the same rate for Comp and for Mechanical Prep, assign one section of the box for those total hours.)

YOUR HOURS

•

12 TIME COSTS

EXAMPLE

• Multiply the total number of project hours in Box 11 by your Hourly Fee Rate to get the Total Project Time Costs.......$2,100
(To simplify the example, an average hourly fee of $60 was used. If you charge different rates for activities, multiply the hours for all activities for which you charge the same rate by that rate. Total all the charges. For example, Concept Development + Client Meetings = 70 hrs x $85/hr = $5,950)

YOUR COSTS

•

11 HIDDEN SURPRISE FACTOR

EXAMPLE

• Multiply the amount in Box 10 by .10 (10%); add that to your total project hours to guard against hidden surprises (accidents, emergencies, problems caused by the client, etc.) ....32 + 3 = 35 hrs
(Build a margin into your estimate to avoid overruns that anger clients or cost you money. The hidden surprise factor used here is 10% because this client has difficulty making final decisions.)

YOUR HOURS

•

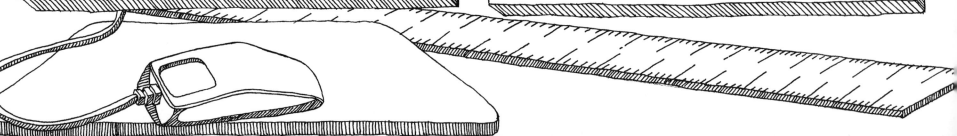

13 URGENCY OF JOB

EXAMPLE

What We Know:
- Deadline is manageable; no overtime
- Time needed ....0 hrs
- Rush charge ....0%/$0

Total Time Required/Total Rush Costs....................0 hrs/$0
- (For a rush project, add your overtime charge or percentage for rush work. Enter here only the cost of the extra charge. For example, at $60, time-and-a-half would cost an extra $30/hour. For 3 hours of overtime, the charge would be $90. If the Total Project Time Cost was $1,200 and your rush charge percentage was 20%, a rush charge on the job would be $240 ($1,200 x .2))

YOUR COSTS

What You Know:
-
- Time needed ...._____hrs
- Rush charge............._____%/$_____

Total Time Required/Total Rush Costs....._____hrs/$_____
-

14 PRODUCTION COSTS

EXAMPLE

What We Know:
- Computer fees (layouts, mechanicals & type) $275
- Supplies...25
- Subtotal $300
- Markup (0%; expenses covered in total fee) 0

  (Not all artists charge markup; whether you do or don't, be consistent in your practice.)
- Total Known Costs..........................$300

Total Production Costs $300

YOUR COSTS

What You Know:
-
-
-
-
- Total Known Costs...............$_____

Total Production Costs...........................$_____

16 TOTAL PROJECT COSTS

EXAMPLE

What We Know:
- Total Project Costs $2,400
- Client wants all rights ....$0 usage fee (The fee is inclusive of cost for usage.)

Total Costs $2,400
- (The more rights a client requests, the higher the fee you should charge. Be very careful if a client asks for "all rights" or a "buyout." The fee for the rights involved, if more than one-time rights, must be negotiated with the client and varies from project to project.)
- Sales Tax (Calculate sales tax only for the final invoice since it has to be figured on actual costs.)

YOUR COSTS

What You Know:
-
-

Total Costs.................$_____
-

-

15 PRODUCTION AND FEE COSTS

EXAMPLE
- Add the dollar amounts in Boxes 12, 13 and 14 to get the total amount of service fees and production costs.........$2,400

YOUR COSTS
-

WORKSHEET 17
SIGNAGE/LARGE SCALE GRAPHICS

This example involves pricing an integrated internal/external signage system for a midsized hospital. Designers charge only for creative and design fees; fabrication and installation is billed directly to the client. However, the cost for both areas is included in the total project cost.

Accurately estimating the cost of any project involves figuring out the cost of the materials and services you'll purchase on behalf of the client as well as the cost of your time. To arrive at an estimate for a job, fill in the amounts requested as you move through the gameboard. Skip boxes that do not apply, but otherwise go in order until you reach the goal. Inside each box, you'll find an example printed on the left and blank spaces on the right for you to use.

START

1 PROJECT TITLE— INTERNAL/EXTERNAL SIGNAGE SYSTEM

Client Name: Marion Hospital
Client Budget: $200,000-400,000
Time Frame: 12 months

2 COMPLEXITY OF JOB

EXAMPLE
What We Know:
- 2-color, internal/external signage
- Internal signage relates to color-coded directionals along corridors
- Designs need approval of hospital board
- Client is opinionated and demanding
- Fired last design firm for failure to meet their needs
- Contract must clearly state kill fee
- Time needed ....25 hrs

Total Time
Required..........................25 hrs

YOUR HOURS
What You Know:
-
-
-
-
-
- Time needed ...._____hrs

Total Time
Required................_____hrs

4 CONCEPT DEVELOPMENT

EXAMPLE
What We Know:
- Master plan of facility includes diagrammatic floor plans and external mapping of signage area
- 2-3 layout designs for signage
- Computer-generated imaging/color output of signs on site
- Time needed ....85 hrs

What We Need:
- Time for final revisions
- Prep time for presentation to board
- Time needed ....75 hrs

Total Time
Required..........................160 hrs

YOUR HOURS
What You Know:
-
-
-
- Time needed ...._____hrs

What You Need:
-
-
- Time needed....................._____hrs

Total Time
Required.................._____hrs

3 INITIAL CLIENT MEETING

EXAMPLE
What We Know:
- Discuss client's design ideas, needs and preferences
- Meeting to include tour of facilities
- Time needed ....5 hrs

What We Need:
- Complete research of all area hospitals after meeting
- Planning and analysis of facility and client needs
- Time needed ....40 hrs

Total Time
Required..........................45 hrs

YOUR HOURS
What You Know:
-
-
- Time needed ...._____hrs

What You Need:
-
-
- Time needed ...._____hrs

Total Time
Required.................._____hrs

5 CLIENT REQUIREMENTS FOR PROJECT

EXAMPLE

What We Know:

- High quality production
- Build in extra time for client hand-holding
- Each approval must go through a committee and board of directors
- Time needed ....25 hrs

Total Time Required..........................**25 hrs**

YOUR HOURS

What You Know:

-
-
-
- Time needed ...._____ hrs

Total Time Required ...._____ **hrs**

6 PREPARING COMPS

EXAMPLE

What We Know:

- Computer-generated color comps of final design selections
- Photos of interior/exterior areas with designs scanned to show application
- Scale model of sample exterior sign
- Presentation to board
- Time needed ....85 hrs

What We Need:

- Color copies of comps mounted for presentation
- Time for additional revisions
- Construction documents for bid solicitation
- Time needed ....55 hrs

Total Time Required..........................**140 hrs**

YOUR HOURS

What You Know:

-
-
-
-
- Time needed ...._____ hrs

What You Need:

-
-
-
- Time needed................_____ hrs

Total Time Required ...._____ **hrs**

TURN PAGE

8 CLIENT MEETINGS

EXAMPLE

What We Know:

- Approve master plan, diagrams, designs
- Approve comps, scale model, revisions, fabrication layouts, prototypes, materials and vinyl samples
- Time needed ....45 hrs

What We Need:

- Approval/change forms for client signature
- Time needed ....18 hrs

Total Time Required..........................**63 hrs**

YOUR HOURS

What You Know:

-
-
- Time needed ...._____ hrs

What You Need:

-
- Time needed ...._____ hrs

Total Time Required.................._____ **hrs**

7 MECHANICAL PREPARATION

EXAMPLE

What We Know:

- Fabricator needs sign layout
- Prepare fabrication and installation schedule
- Approve templates, prototypes, sample materials, finished sign sample, and vinyl-cut-letter samples
- Supervise and inspect installations
- Inspect completed installation site
- Time needed ....45 hrs

What We Need:

- Punch list of errors in signs or installation; client Standards Manual
- Time needed ....33 hrs

Total Time Required .....**78 hrs**

YOUR HOURS

What You Know:

-
-
-
-
- Time needed ...._____ hrs

What You Need:

-
- Time needed ...._____ hrs

Total Time Required....._____ **hrs**

WORKSHEET 17 CONTINUED

9 CLERICAL/ADMINISTRATIVE WORK

EXAMPLE

What We Know:
- Prepare price estimate, schedule and billing account
- Prepare quarterly project reviews
- Time needed ....5 hrs

What We Need:
- Bids (price/schedule) confirmation from fabricator
- Time needed ....2 hrs

Total Time Required ....7 hrs

YOUR HOURS

What You Know:
-
-
- Time needed ...._____hrs

What You Need:
-
- Time needed ...._____hrs

Total Time Required ...._____hrs

12 TIME COSTS

EXAMPLE
- Multiply the total number of project hours in Box 11 by your Hourly Fee Rate to get the Total Project Time Costs.......$50,745 (An average hourly fee of $85 was used because this is a specialized design service. If you charge different rates for activities, multiply the hours for all activities for which you charge the same rate by that rate. Total all the charges. For example, Concept Development + Client Meetings = 70 hrs x $85/hr = $5,950)

YOUR COSTS
-

11 HIDDEN SURPRISE FACTOR

EXAMPLE
- Multiply the amount in Box 10 by .10 (10%); add that to Box 10 to guard against hidden surprises (accidents, emergencies, problems caused by the client, etc.).................543 + 54 = 597 hrs (Build a margin into your estimates to avoid cost overruns that anger clients or cost you money. The hidden surprise factor used here is 10% because this client is clearly going to be demanding to work with. It's a good idea to go to 15% on a project you've never done before, but a 5% security blanket may be enough in many cases.)

YOUR HOURS
-

10 TOTAL PROJECT HOURS

EXAMPLE
- Add your hours in Boxes 1-9 to estimate Total Project Hours.....................543 hrs (If you charge different rates for activities, divide the box into sections, one section per rate. For example, if you have the same rate for Comp and for Mechanical Prep, assign one section of the box for those total hours.)

YOUR HOURS
-

13 URGENCY OF JOB

EXAMPLE
What We Know:
- Deadline is manageable; no overtime
- Time needed ....0 hrs
- Rush charge ....0%/$0

Total Time Required/Total
Rush Costs ....0 hrs/$0
- (For a rush project, add your overtime charge or percentage for rush work. Enter here only the cost of the extra charge. For example, at $60, time-and-a-half would cost an extra $30/hour. For 3 hours of overtime, the charge would be $90. If the Total Project Time Cost was $1,200 and your rush charge percentage was 20%, a rush charge on the job would be $240 ($1,200 x .2))

YOUR COSTS
What You Know:
-
- Time needed ...._____hrs
- Rush charge............._____%/$_____

Total Time Required/Total
Rush Costs....._____hrs/$_____
-

16 TOTAL PROJECT COSTS

GOAL

EXAMPLE
What We Know:
- Total Project Costs....................$326,840
- Fee covers all rights; not copyright ......$0 usage fee

Total Costs $326,840
- (The more rights a client requests, the higher the fee you should charge. Be very careful if a client asks for "all rights" or a "buyout." The fee for the rights involved, if more than one-time rights, must be negotiated with the client and varies from project to project.)
- Sales Tax
  (Calculate sales tax only for the final invoice since it has to be figured on actual costs.)

YOUR COSTS
What You Know:
-
-

Total Costs.................$_____
-

-

14 PRODUCTION COSTS

EXAMPLE
What We Know:
- Fabrication/installation $250,000
- Travel 275
- Supplies..450
- Color copies 45
- Faxes 75
- Blueprints 150
- Subtotal $250,995
- Markup (0%) 0
  (Not all artists charge markup; whether you do or don't, be consistent in your practice.)
- Total Known Costs....................$250,995

What We Need:
- 10% margin for extra costs....$25,099.50

Total Production
Costs $276,094.50

YOUR COSTS
What You Know:
-
-
-
-
-
-
-
-

- Total Known Costs...........$_____

What You Need:
-

Total Production
Costs ....$_____

15 PRODUCTION AND FEE COSTS

EXAMPLE
- Add the dollar amounts in Boxes 12, 13 and 14 to get the total amount of service fees and production costs......$326,840

YOUR COSTS
-

WORKSHEET 18

PACKAGING

A packaging assignment can range from redesigning an existing package to the naming and an identity for a whole line of products. This example is based on developing a brand identity and packaging for a product.

Accurately estimating the cost of any project involves figuring out the cost of the materials and services you'll purchase on behalf of the client as well as the cost of your time. To arrive at an estimate for a job, fill in the amounts requested as you move through the gameboard. Skip boxes that do not apply, but otherwise go in order until you reach the goal. Inside each box, you'll find an example printed on the left and blank spaces on the right for you to use.

START

1 PROJECT TITLE— CONSUMER PRODUCT PACKAGE DESIGN

Client Name: California Fruit Juice Corp.
Client Budget: $19,000-21,000
Time Frame: 2 months

2 COMPLEXITY OF JOB

EXAMPLE

What We Know:
- Develop identity and design packaging for 5 fruit juice containers
- Mass market distribution
- 3-colors, quart and half-gallon sizes
- Requires extensive market research and competitive analysis
- Focus groups conducted before final design is selected
- Time needed ....20 hrs

Total Time
Required............................**20 hrs**

YOUR HOURS

What You Know:
-
-
-
-
-
- Time needed ...._____hrs

Total Time
Required.............._____hrs

4 CONCEPT DEVELOPMENT

EXAMPLE

What We Know:
- Develop 10 rough thumbnails for each container
- Select 2-3 color thumbnails; do computer roughs to size
- Time needed ....55 hrs

What We Need:
- Focus groups prior to final selection
- Revision time following final selection
- Time needed ....30 hrs

Total Time
Required..........................**85 hrs**

YOUR HOURS

What You Know:
-
-
- Time needed ...._____hrs

What You Need:
-
-
- Time needed ...._____hrs

Total Time
Required................._____hrs

3 INITIAL CLIENT MEETING

EXAMPLE

What We Know:
- The product is named
- Client has definite ideas about the design look
- Time needed ....3 hrs

What We Need:
- Packaging samples from client's other product lines
- Price point, distribution and marketing plans
- Time needed ....3 hrs

Total Time
Required............................**6 hrs**

YOUR HOURS

What You Know:
-
-
- Time needed ...._____hrs

What You Need:
-
-
- Time needed ...._____hrs

Total Time
Required................._____hrs

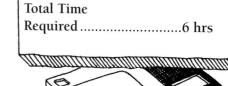

5 CLIENT REQUIREMENTS FOR PROJECT

EXAMPLE

What We Know:
- Client will handle printing
- Focus groups billed to client
- Highly competitive area; product must be distinctive
- Research will be time-intensive
- Time needed ....20 hrs

Total Time Required...........................20 hrs

YOUR HOURS

What You Know:
-
-
-

-
- Time needed ...._____hrs

Total Time Required ...._____hrs

8 CLIENT MEETINGS

EXAMPLE

What We Know:
- Approve thumbnail roughs
- Review results of focus groups
- Presentation
- Approve electronic keylines, reflective art and match prints
- Time needed ....10 hrs

Total Time Required...........................10 hrs

YOUR HOURS

What You Know:
-
-
-
-

- Time needed ...._____hrs

Total Time Required..................._____hrs

TURN PAGE

6 PREPARING COMPS

EXAMPLE

What We Know:
- Tight computer renderings of selected designs mounted on gray board
- 3-D mock up of each container
- Presentation to brand manager, sales and marketing teams
- Time needed ....25 hrs

What We Need:
- Packets for presentations
- Color copies of comps
- Printer to provide sample die vinyl
- Time needed ....5 hrs

Total Time Required...........................30 hrs

YOUR HOURS

What You Know:
-
-
-

- Time needed ...._____hrs

What You Need:
-
-
-

- Time needed ...._____hrs

Total Time Required.............._____hrs

7 MECHANICAL PREPARATION

EXAMPLE

What We Know:
- Produce electronic keylines for 5 carton designs in 3 colors
- Send logo to color
- Scitex corrections and trappings to be done
- Approve match prints
- Time needed ....45 hrs

What We Need:
- Request bids (prices/schedules) from vendors/subcontractors
- Time needed ....4 hrs

Total Time Required.......................49 hrs

YOUR HOURS

What You Know:
-
-
-

- Time needed ...._____hrs

What You Need:
-

- Time needed ...._____hrs

Total Time Required ...._____hrs

WORKSHEET 18 *CONTINUED*

9 CLERICAL/ADMINISTRATIVE WORK

EXAMPLE

What We Know:
- Prepare price estimate and schedule
- Set up billing account
- Time needed ....3 hrs

What We Need:
- Bid confirmation from vendors/subcontractors
- Time needed ....1 hr

Total Time Required.............................**4 hrs**

YOUR HOURS

What You Know:
-
-
- Time needed..............._____hrs

What You Need:
-
- Time needed..............._____hrs

Total Time Required ...._____**hrs**

10 TOTAL PROJECT HOURS

EXAMPLE
- Add your hours in Boxes 1-9 to estimate Total Project Hours ....224 hrs
  (If you charge different rates for activities, divide the box into sections, one section per rate. For example, if you have the same rate for Comp and for Mechanical Prep, assign one section of the box for those total hours.)

YOUR HOURS
-

12 TIME COSTS

EXAMPLE
- Multiply the total number of project hours in Box 11 by your Hourly Fee Rate to get the Total Project Time Costs.......$15,480
  (To simplify the example, an average hourly fee of $60 was used. If you charge different rates for activities, multiply the hours for all activities for which you charge the same rate by that rate. Total all the charges. For example, Concept Development + Client Meetings = 70 hrs x $85/hr = $5,950)

YOUR COSTS
-

11 HIDDEN SURPRISE FACTOR

EXAMPLE
- Multiply the amount in Box 10 by .15 (15%); add that to Box 10 to guard against hidden surprises (accidents, emergencies, problems caused by the client, etc.). ....224 + 34 = 258 hrs
  (Build a margin into your estimate to avoid cost overruns that anger clients or cost you money. The hidden surprise factor used here is 15% because this client is clearly going to be difficult to work with; it's also a good idea to go to this level on a project you've never done before. A 5% security blanket may be enough in many cases.)

YOUR HOURS
-

13 URGENCY OF JOB

EXAMPLE

What We Know:
- Deadline is manageable; no overtime
- Time needed ....0 hrs
- Rush charge ....0%/$0

Total Time Required/Total Rush Costs ....0 hrs/$0
- (For a rush project, add your overtime charge or percentage for rush work. Enter here only the cost of the extra charge. For example, at $60, time-and-a-half would cost an extra $30/hour. For 3 hours of overtime, the charge would be $90. If the Total Project Time Cost was $1,200 and your rush charge percentage was 20%, a rush charge on the job would be $240 ($1,200 x .2))

YOUR COSTS

What You Know:
-
- Time needed ...._____hrs
- Rush charge............_____%/$_____

Total Time Required/Total Rush Costs....._____hrs/$_____
-

14 PRODUCTION COSTS

EXAMPLE

What We Know:
- Service bureau $450
- Separations....................................1,000
- Scitex..1,500
- Cartons for mock-ups 70
- Supplies...250
- Subtotal $3,270
- Markup (15%) 491

  (Not all artists charge markup; whether you do or don't, be consistent in your practice.)
- Total Known Costs $3,761

What We Need:
- 10% margin for extra costs..............$376

Total Production Costs $4,137

YOUR COSTS

What You Know:
-
-
-
-
-
-
-
- Total Known Costs ....$_____

What You Need:
-

Total Production Costs ....$_____

16 TOTAL PROJECT COSTS

GOAL

EXAMPLE

What We Know:
- Total Project Costs.................$19,617
- Fee covers all rights........$1,000 usage fee

Total Costs..................$20,617
- (The more rights a client requests, the higher the fee you should charge. Be very careful if a client asks for "all rights" or a "buyout." The fee for the rights involved, if more than one-time rights, must be negotiated with the client and varies from project to project.)
- Sales Tax
  (Calculate sales tax only for the final invoice since it has to be figured on actual costs.)

YOUR COSTS

What You Know:
-
-

Total Costs................$_____
-

15 PRODUCTION AND FEE COSTS

EXAMPLE
- Add the dollar amounts in Boxes 12, 13 and 14 to get the total amount of service fees and production costs...........$19,617

YOUR COSTS
-

WORKSHEET 19
POSTER

This example involves pricing design and illustration for a 4-color poster. Posters are usually produced and priced for a one-time usage only. Geographical distribution is also a consideration when determining the usage fee.

Accurately estimating the cost of any project involves figuring out the cost of the materials and services you'll purchase on behalf of the client as well as the cost of your time. To arrive at an estimate for a job, fill in the amounts requested as you move through the gameboard. Skip boxes that do not apply, but otherwise go in order until you reach the goal. Inside each box, you'll find an example printed on the left and blank spaces on the right for you to use.

START

1 PROJECT TITLE—POSTER DESIGN & ILLUSTRATION FOR NYC JAZZ FESTIVAL

Client Name: Martin Masson Promotions
Client Budget: $5,000-8,000
Time Frame: 3 weeks

2 COMPLEXITY OF JOB

EXAMPLE
What We Know:
• 4-color poster for 1-day jazz festival
• Stylized illustration of concert performers
• Client has photograph references for illustrations
• Research posters used for other concerts
• Client is demanding and difficult to work with
• Client prone to make last-minute changes
• Time needed ....2 hrs

Total Time
Required............................**2 hrs**

YOUR HOURS
What You Know:
•
•
•
•
•
•
• Time needed................_____hrs

Total Time
Required................_____**hrs**

4 CONCEPT DEVELOPMENT

EXAMPLE
What We Know:
• Client wants 3 well-developed sketches for illustrations and designs
• Time needed ....15 hrs

What We Need:
• Paper samples
• Typeface samples
• Time needed ....1 hr

Total Time
Required............................**16 hrs**

YOUR HOURS
What You Know:
•
• Time needed ...._____hrs

What You Need:
•
•
• Time needed...................._____hrs

Total Time
Required................_____**hrs**

3 INITIAL CLIENT MEETING

EXAMPLE
What We Know:
• Client wants to see samples of our illustrations and poster designs
• Discuss audience demographics
• Time needed ....2 hrs

What We Need:
• Review other festival posters before meeting
• Research on performers
• Time needed ....3 hrs

Total Time
Required............................**5 hrs**

YOUR HOURS
What You Know:
•
•
• Time needed ...._____hrs

What You Need:
•
•
• Time needed ...._____hrs

Total Time
Required................_____**hrs**

5 CLIENT REQUIREMENTS FOR PROJECT

EXAMPLE

What We Know:
- Slick, dynamic piece required
- Time needed ....5 hrs

Total Time Required..........................5 hrs

YOUR HOURS

What You Know:
-
- Time needed ...._____hrs

Total Time Required ...._____hrs

6 PREPARING COMPS

EXAMPLE

What We Know:
- We can go straight from approved sketch to completed illustration
- Make any revisions of approved layout design and develop into full-size, color comp
- Paste copy of finished illustration into layout comp
- Time needed ....21 hrs

What We Need:
- Client wants 5 color copies of comp
- Allow time for revisions
- Time needed ....5 hrs

Total Time Required..........................26 hrs

YOUR HOURS

What You Know:
-
-
-
- Time needed ...._____hrs

What You Need:
-
-
- Time needed ...._____hrs

Total Time Required ...._____hrs

8 CLIENT MEETINGS

TURN PAGE

EXAMPLE

What We Know:
- Approve initial sketches, layout designs, final illustration and comp
- Approve mechanical
- Approve Color-Key and color separation
- Time needed ....5 hrs

What We Need:
- Approval/change form for client signature
- Time needed ....1 hr

Total Time Required..........................6 hrs

YOUR HOURS

What You Know:
-
-
-
- Time needed ...._____hrs

What You Need:
-
- Time needed ...._____hrs

Total Time Required................_____hrs

7 MECHANICAL PREPARATION

EXAMPLE

What We Know:
- Type spec finished layout
- Color separate illustration
- Paste-up type, prepare color overlays and mask for photo
- Approve color proof and separation
- Approve press proof
- Time needed ....7 hrs

What We Need:
- Request bids (prices/schedules) from vendors/subcontractors
- Time needed ....2 hrs

Total Time Required ....9 hrs

YOUR HOURS

What You Know:
-
-
-
-
-
- Time needed................_____hrs

What You Need:
-
- Time needed................_____hrs

Total Time Required ...._____hrs

WORKSHEET 19 *CONTINUED*

9 CLERICAL/ADMINISTRATIVE WORK

EXAMPLE

What We Know:
• Prepare price estimate and schedule
• Set up billing account
• Time needed ....2 hrs

What We Need:
• Bid confirmation from vendors/subcontractors
• Time needed ....1 hr

Total Time
Required ....3 hrs

YOUR HOURS

What You Know:
•
•
• Time needed ...._____hrs

What You Need:
•
• Time needed ...._____hrs

Total Time
Required ...._____hrs

10 TOTAL PROJECT HOURS

EXAMPLE

• Add your hours in Boxes 1-9 to estimate Total Project Hours ....72 hrs
(If you charge different rates for activities, divide the box into sections, one section per rate. For example, if you have the same rate for Comp and for Mechanical Prep, assign one section of the box for those total hours.)

YOUR HOURS
•

12 TIME COSTS

EXAMPLE

• Multiply the total number of project hours in Box 11 by your Hourly Fee Rate to get the Total Project Time Costs $4,740
(To simplify the example, an average hourly fee of $60 has been used. If you charge different rates for activities, multiply the hours for all activities for which you charge the same rate by that rate. Total all the charges. For example, Concept Development + Client Meetings = 70 hrs x $85/hr = $5,950)

YOUR COSTS
•

11 HIDDEN SURPRISE FACTOR

EXAMPLE

• Multiply the amount in Box 10 by .10 (10%); add that to Box 10 to guard against hidden surprises (accidents, emergencies, problems caused by the client, etc.)...................72 + 7 = 79 hrs
(Build a margin into your estimate to avoid cost overruns that anger clients or cost you money. The hidden surprise factor used here is 10% because this client is clearly going to be difficult to work with. It's a good idea to go to 15% on a project you've never done before, but a 5% security blanket may be enough in many cases.)

YOUR HOURS
•

13 URGENCY OF JOB

EXAMPLE
What We Know:
- Deadline is tight but manageable
- Time needed ....4 hrs
- Rush charge $30/hr

Total Time Required/Total
Rush Costs ....4 hrs/$120
- (For a rush project, add your overtime charge or percentage for rush work. Enter here only the cost of the extra charge. For example, at $60, time-and-a-half would cost an extra $30/hour. For 3 hours of overtime, the charge would be $90. If the Total Project Time Cost was $1,200 and your rush charge percentage was 20%, a rush charge on the job would be $240 ($1,200 x .2))

YOUR COSTS
What You Know:
-
- Time needed ...._____hrs
- Rush charge..................$_____/hr

Total Time Required/Total
Rush Costs....._____hrs/$_____
-

14 PRODUCTION COSTS

EXAMPLE
What We Know:
- Typesetting $120
- Printing...1,500
- Color separation 375
- Supplies...50
- Subtotal $2,045
- Markup (15%) 307
  (Not all artists charge markup; whether you do or don't, be consistent in your practice.)
- Total Known Costs $2,352

What We Need:
- 10% margin for extra costs..............$235

**Total Production
Costs $2,587**

YOUR COSTS
What You Know:
-
-
-
-
-
-
- Total Known Costs..............$_____

What You Need:
-

**Total Production
Costs ....$_____**

16 TOTAL PROJECT COSTS

EXAMPLE
What We Know:
- Total Project Costs........................$7,447
- One-time use within local geographical area................................$250 usage fee
- If design is to be used for other purposes, price will be renegotiated.

Total Costs $7,697
- (The more rights a client requests, the higher the fee you should charge. Be very careful if a client asks for "all rights" or a "buyout." The fee for the rights involved, if more than one-time rights, must be negotiated with the client and varies from project to project.)
- Sales Tax
  (Calculate sales tax only for the final invoice since it has to be figured on actual costs.)

YOUR COSTS
What You Know:
-
-
-

Total Costs.................$_____
-

-

15 PRODUCTION AND FEE COSTS

EXAMPLE
- Add the dollar amounts in Boxes 12, 13 and 14 to get the total amount of service fees and production costs..........$7,447

YOUR COSTS
-

WORKSHEET 20

NEWSPAPER AD

This example prices a full-page b&w ad with an illustration for a local newspaper. Price a newspaper ad on the time involved to produce it, not on the newspaper's circulation size and geographical distribution.

Accurately estimating the cost of any project involves figuring out the cost of the materials and services you'll purchase on behalf of the client as well as the cost of your time. To arrive at an estimate for a job, fill in the amounts requested as you move through the gameboard. Skip boxes that do not apply, but otherwise go in order until you reach the goal. Inside each box, you'll find an example printed on the left and blank spaces on the right for you to use.

1 PROJECT TITLE— NEWSPAPER AD

Client Name: JRS Advertising Agency
Client Budget: $6,000-7,000
Time Frame: 2 weeks

2 COMPLEXITY OF JOB

EXAMPLE

What We Know:
- Full-page, b&w ad for local newspaper
- Half-page tonal illustration included
- Agency to provide headline and copy
- Requires research of competitive ad designs
- Time needed ....2 hrs

Total Time
Required............................2 hrs

YOUR HOURS

What You Know:
- •
- •
- •
- •
- Time needed ...._____hrs

Total Time
Required.............._____hrs

4 CONCEPT DEVELOPMENT

EXAMPLE

What We Know:
- Client wants 3 tissue roughs for ad layouts, and 2-3 rough sketches for illustration concept
- Time needed ....20 hrs

What We Need:
- Reference photos for illustration
- Time for revisions to selected ad layout
- Time needed ....12 hrs

Total Time
Required............................32 hrs

YOUR HOURS

What You Know:
- •
- Time needed ...._____hrs

What You Need:
- •
- •
- Time needed...................._____hrs

Total Time
Required................._____hrs

3 INITIAL CLIENT MEETING

EXAMPLE

What We Know:
- Art director has sketches we can work from
- Ask client about target market demographics
- Time needed....................................1 hr

What We Need:
- • Samples of the ads the agency's client has run previously
- Time needed.................................1 hr

Total Time
Required............................2 hrs

YOUR HOURS

What You Know:
- •
- •
- Time needed ...._____hrs

What You Need:
- •
- Time needed ...._____hrs

Total Time
Required................._____hrs

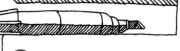

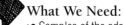

5 CLIENT REQUIREMENTS FOR PROJECT

EXAMPLE

What We Know:
• High-end production required
• Turnaround time is tight
• Client is finicky and prone to making lots of changes
• Time needed ....5 hrs

Total Time Required ....5 hrs

YOUR HOURS

What You Know:
•
•
•
• Time needed ...._____hrs

Total Time Required ...._____hrs

6 PREPARING COMPS

EXAMPLE

What We Know:
• Complete final illustration from selected sketches
• Full-size, computer-generated ad layout with illustration scanned into position
• Time needed ....12 hrs

What We Need:
• 10 mounted copies of comp for agency presentation to client
• Time for final revisions
• Time needed ....4 hrs

Total Time Required ....16 hrs

YOUR HOURS

What You Know:
•
•
• Time needed ...._____hrs

What You Need:
•
•
• Time needed..................._____hrs

Total Time Required ...._____hrs

TURN PAGE

8 CLIENT MEETINGS

EXAMPLE

What We Know:
• Approval of concept, comp, art and mechanical
• Revision meeting
• Delivery of stat and mechanical to agency
• Time needed ....5 hrs

What We Need:
• Approval/change form for client
• Time needed ....1 hr

Total Time Required ....6 hrs

YOUR HOURS

What You Know:
•
•
• Time needed ...._____hrs

What You Need:
•
• Time needed................._____hrs

Total Time Required ...._____hrs

7 MECHANICAL PREPARATION

EXAMPLE

What We Know:
• Line screen for illustration
• Paste-up ad and illustration halftone
• Proof mechanical
• Time needed ....8 hrs

What We Need:
• Get stat of ad for agency to send to publication
• Build in time for final revisions
• Time needed ....5 hrs

Total Time Required ....13 hrs

YOUR HOURS

What You Know:
•
•
•
• Time needed ...._____hrs

What You Need:
•
• Time needed...................._____hrs

Total Time Required ...._____hrs

WORKSHEET 20 *CONTINUED*

9 CLERICAL/ADMINISTRATIVE WORK

EXAMPLE

What We Know:
• Prepare price estimate and schedule
• Set up billing account
• Time needed ....2 hrs

What We Need:
• Contract must clearly state kill fee
• Time needed ....1 hr

Total Time
Required ....3 hrs

YOUR HOURS

What You Know:
•

•

• Time needed..............._____hrs

What You Need:
•

• Time needed..............._____hrs

Total Time
Required ...._____hrs

10 TOTAL PROJECT HOURS

EXAMPLE
• Add your hours in Boxes 1-9 to estimate
the Total Project Hours. ....79 hrs
(If you charge different rates for activities,
divide the box into sections, one section
per rate. For example, if you have the
same rate for Comp and for Mechanical
Prep, assign one section of the box for
those total hours.)

YOUR HOURS
•

12 TIME COSTS

EXAMPLE
• Multiply the total number of project hours
in Box 11 by your Hourly Fee Rate to get
the Total Project Time Costs.......$5,220
(To simplify the example, an average
hourly fee of $60 was used. If you charge
different rates for activities, multiply the
hours for all activities for which you
charge the same rate by that rate. Total all
the charges. For example, Concept
Development + Client Meetings = 70 hrs x
$85/hr = $5,950)

YOUR COSTS
•

11 HIDDEN SURPRISE FACTOR

EXAMPLE
• Multiply the amount in Box 10 by .10
(10%); add that to your total project
hours to guard against hidden surprises
(accidents, emergencies, problems caused
by the client, etc.)........79 + 8 = 87 hrs
(Build a margin into your estimate to
avoid cost overruns that anger clients
or cost you money. The hidden surprise
factor used here is 10% because this
client is going to be difficult to work with.
It's a good idea to go to 15% on a project
you've never done before, but a 5%
security blanket may be enough in many
cases.)

YOUR HOURS
•

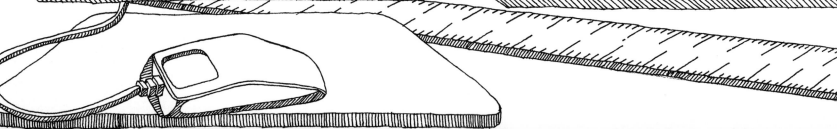

13 URGENCY OF JOB

EXAMPLE

What We Know:
- Deadline is tight; overtime likely
- Time needed ....5 hrs
- Rush charge $30/hr

**Total Time Required/Total
Rush Costs ....5 hrs/$150**
- (For a rush project, add your overtime charge or percentage for rush work. Enter here only the cost of the extra charge. For example, at $60, time-and-a-half would cost an extra $30/hour. For 3 hours of overtime, the charge would be $90. If the Total Project Time Cost was $1,200 and your rush charge percentage was 20%, a rush charge on the job would be $240 ($1,200 x .2))

YOUR COSTS

What You Know:
-
- Time needed ...._____hrs
- Rush charge ....$_____/hr

**Total Time Required/Total
Rush Costs...._____hrs/$_____**
-

16 TOTAL PROJECT COSTS

GOAL

EXAMPLE

What We Know:
- Total Project Costs $5,865
- Full rights buyout.........$600 usage fee

Total Costs $6,465
- (The more rights a client requests, the higher the fee you should charge. Be very careful if a client asks for "all rights" or a "buyout." The fee for the rights involved, if more than one-time rights, must be negotiated with the client and varies from project to project.)
- Sales Tax
  (Calculate sales tax only for the final invoice since it has to be figured on actual costs.)

YOUR COSTS

What You Know:
-
-

Total Costs.................$_____
-

14 PRODUCTION COSTS

EXAMPLE

What We Know:
- Computer fees...................................$150
- Typesetting 200
- Stats & Linescreen...............................55
- Materials 25
- Subtotal $430
- Markup (15%) 65
  (Not all artists charge markup; whether you do or don't, be consistent in your practice.)
- Total Known Costs...........................$495

**Total Production
Costs $495**

YOUR COSTS

What You Know:
-
-
-
-
-
-
- Total Known Costs...............$_____

**Total Production
Costs.........................$_____**

15 PRODUCTION AND FEE COSTS

EXAMPLE
- Add the dollar amounts in Boxes 12, 13 and 14 to get the total amount of service fees and production costs.............$5,865

YOUR COSTS
-

WORKSHEET 21
MAGAZINE AD

This worksheet features a full-page, 4-color ad introducing a new product line. For publication work, some designers adjust their prices based on a publication's circulation and distribution, a practice that devalues a designer's work.

Accurately estimating the cost of any project involves figuring out the cost of the materials and services you'll purchase on behalf of the client as well as the cost of your time. To arrive at an estimate for a job, fill in the amounts requested as you move through the gameboard. Skip boxes that do not apply, but otherwise go in order until you reach the goal. Inside each box, you'll find an example printed on the left and blank spaces on the right for you to use.

1 PROJECT TITLE— MAGAZINE AD

Client Name: Trintron, Inc.
Client Budget: $4,500-6,500
Time Frame: 2 months

2 COMPLEXITY OF JOB

EXAMPLE

What We Know:
- Design a full-page, 4-color ad displaying new product line for a consumer magazine
- Includes 3 color photos
- We provide copy & headline, will subcontract to writer
- Research competitive products and ads
- Time needed ....2 hrs

Total Time
Required.............................2 hrs

YOUR HOURS

What You Know:
-
-
-
-
- Time needed ...._____hrs

Total Time
Required................._____hrs

4 CONCEPT DEVELOPMENT

EXAMPLE

What We Know:
- Client wants 3 tissue roughs of ad design in color
- Client wants 3 typeset headlines and copy roughs
- Photographer will follow our sketches for art direction
- Time needed ....25 hrs

What We Need:
- 10 color copies of ad concepts
- 10 copies of heads/copy
- Time needed ....2 hrs

Total Time
Required...........................27 hrs

YOUR HOURS

What You Know:
-
-
-
- Time needed ...._____hrs

What You Need:
-
-
- Time needed..................._____hrs

Total Time
Required................._____hrs

3 INITIAL CLIENT MEETING

EXAMPLE

What We Know:
- Get publication's media kit
- Review research on competitors
- Time needed ....6 hrs

What We Need:
- Product demonstration
- Product spec sheet
- Time needed ....3 hrs

Total Time
Required.............................9 hrs

YOUR HOURS

What You Know:
-
-
- Time needed ...._____hrs

What You Need:
-
-
- Time needed ...._____hrs

Total Time
Required................._____hrs

5 CLIENT REQUIREMENTS FOR PROJECT

EXAMPLE

What We Know:
- High-quality production required
- Client prone to making many changes
- Time needed ....5 hrs

Total Time
Required ....5 hrs

YOUR HOURS

What You Know:
-
-
- Time needed ...._____hrs

Total Time
Required ...._____hrs

TURN PAGE

8 CLIENT MEETINGS

EXAMPLE

What We Know:
- Approval of initial ideas
- Approval of comp, illustration, copy and mechanical
- Selection of photos
- Time needed ....6 hrs

What We Need:
- Approval/change form for client signature
- Time needed ....1 hr

Total Time
Required ....7 hrs

YOUR HOURS

What You Know:
-
-
-
- Time needed ...._____hrs

What You Need:
-
- Time needed ...._____hrs

Total Time
Required ...._____hrs

6 PREPARING COMPS

EXAMPLE

What We Know:
- Revisions needed on selected layout
- Computer-generated full-color comp
- Art direct photo shoot
- Finalize copy and head
- Complete spot illustration
- Time needed ....15 hrs

What We Need:
- Time for final revisions
- Client approval of photos
- Time needed ....3 hrs

Total Time
Required ....18 hrs

YOUR HOURS

What You Know:
-
-
-
-
-
- Time needed ...._____hrs

What You Need:
-
-
- Time needed ...._____hrs

Total Time
Required ...._____hrs

7 MECHANICAL PREPARATION

EXAMPLE

What We Know:
- Computer-generate and typeset finished ad
- Handle color separations
- Stat spot illustration
- Prepare board; paste-up and proof mechanical
- Get film negs for publication
- Time needed ....7 hrs

What We Need:
- Client approval of mechanical
- Time needed ....1 hr

Total Time
Required ....8 hrs

YOUR HOURS

What You Know:
-
-
-
-
- Time needed ...._____hrs

What You Need:
-
- Time needed ...._____hrs

Total Time
Required ...._____hrs

WORKSHEET 21 *CONTINUED*

9 CLERICAL/ADMINISTRATIVE WORK

EXAMPLE

What We Know:
- Prepare price estimate and schedule
- Set up billing account
- Time needed ....2 hrs

**Total Time
Required ....2 hrs**

YOUR HOURS

What You Know:
-
-
- Time needed..............._____hrs

**Total Time
Required ...._____hrs**

10 TOTAL PROJECT HOURS

EXAMPLE
- Add your hours in Boxes 1-9 to estimate the Total Project Hours ....78 hrs
(If you charge different rates for activities, divide the box into sections, one section per rate. For example, if you have the same rate for Comp and for Mechanical Prep, assign one section of the box for those total hours.)

YOUR HOURS
-

12 TIME COSTS

EXAMPLE
- Multiply the total number of project hours in Box 11 by your Hourly Fee Rate to get the Total Project Time Costs.........$5,160
(To simplify the example, an average hourly fee of $60 was used. If you charge different rates for activities, multiply the hours for all activities for which you charge the same rate by that rate. Total all the charges. For example, Concept Development + Client Meetings = 70 hrs x $85/hr = $5,950)

YOUR COSTS
-

11 HIDDEN SURPRISE FACTOR

EXAMPLE
- Multiply the amount in Box 10 by .10 (10%); add that to your total project hours to guard against hidden surprises (accidents, emergencies, problems caused by the client, etc.) ....78 + 8 = 86 hrs
(Build a margin into your estimate to avoid overruns that anger your clients or cost you money. The hidden surprise factor used here is 10% because this client is going to be difficult to work with. It's a good idea to go to 15% on a project you've never done before, but a 5% security blanket may be enough in many cases.)

YOUR HOURS
-

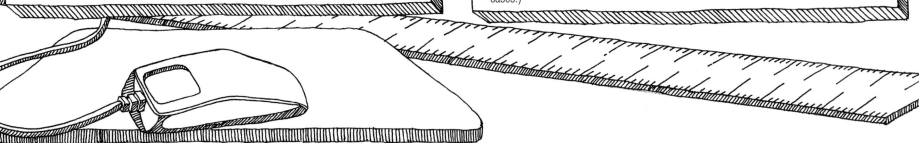

13 URGENCY OF JOB

EXAMPLE
What We Know:
- Deadline is manageable; no overtime
- Time needed ....0 hrs
- Rush charge ....0%/$0

Total Time Required/Total Rush Costs ....0 hrs/$0
- (For a rush project, add your overtime charge or percentage for rush work. Enter here only the cost of the extra charge. For example, at $60, time-and-a-half would cost an extra $30/hour. For 3 hours of overtime, the charge would be $90. If the Total Project Time Cost was $1,200 and your rush charge percentage was 20%, a rush charge on the job would be $240 ($1,200 x .2))

YOUR COSTS
What You Know:
-
  - Time needed ...._____hrs
  - Rush charge ...._____%/$_____

Total Time Required/Total Rush Costs ...._____hrs/$_____
-

16 TOTAL PROJECT COSTS

EXAMPLE
What We Know:
- Fee covers all rights for specified use ....$0 usage fee

Total Costs $6,488
- (The more rights a client requests, the higher the fee you should charge. Be very careful if a client asks for "all rights" or a "buyout." The fee for the rights involved, if more than one-time rights, must be negotiated with the client and varies from project to project.)

- Sales Tax
  (Calculate sales tax only for the final invoice since it has to be figured on actual costs.)

YOUR COSTS
What You Know:
-

Total Costs................$_____
-

-

14 PRODUCTION COSTS

EXAMPLE
What We Know:
- Typesetting & computer usage.........$135
- Photography 500
- Ad separation.....................................375
- Stats..65
- Film negatives.....................................45
- Supplies...35
- Subtotal $1,155
- Markup (15%) 173
  (Not all artists charge markup; whether you do or don't, be consistent in your practice.)
- Total Known Costs.........................$1,328

Total Production Costs $1,328

YOUR COSTS
What You Know:
-
-
-
-
-
-
-
-
- Total Known Costs............$_____

Total Production Costs ....$_____

15 PRODUCTION AND FEE COSTS

EXAMPLE
- Add the dollar amounts in Boxes 12, 13 and 14 to get the total amount of service fees and production costs.........$6,488

YOUR COSTS
-

WORKSHEET 22

BILLBOARD/PUBLIC TRANSIT AD

In this billboard/transit sign design project, the designer is only responsible for creative production. Since the running of ads such as these implies a time limit, that is factored in when determining usage fees and restrictions.

Accurately estimating the cost of any project involves figuring out the cost of the materials and services you'll purchase on behalf of the client as well as the cost of your time. To arrive at an estimate for a job, fill in the amounts requested as you move through the gameboard. Skip boxes that do not apply, but otherwise go in order until you reach the goal. Inside each box, you'll find an example printed on the left and blank spaces on the right for you to use.

START

1 PROJECT TITLE— PROMOTIONAL BILLBOARDS & PUBLIC TRANSIT AD

Client Name: Bright Day
Alcohol Rehabilitation Center
Client Budget: $5,000-8,000
Time Frame: 1 month

2 COMPLEXITY OF JOB

EXAMPLE

What We Know:
- 4-color billboard and public transit ad
- Client has photos
- Requires competition research
- Camera-ready art only; client will purchase space
- Client is demanding and temperamental
- Build in extra time for unexpected client changes
- Time needed ....3 hrs

**Total Time
Required**............................3 hrs

YOUR HOURS

What You Know:
-
-
-
-
-
-
- Time needed ...._____hrs

**Total Time
Required**..............._____hrs

4 CONCEPT DEVELOPMENT

EXAMPLE

What We Know:
- 3 tissue roughs of design concepts for each format
- 3 to 5 sample headlines for each sign
- Time needed ....9 hrs

What We Need:
- Get billboard/transit ad sizes/finished art specifications
- Time needed ....2 hrs

**Total Time
Required**............................11 hrs

YOUR HOURS

What You Know:
-
-
- Time needed ...._____hrs

What You Need:
-
- Time needed...................._____hrs

**Total Time
Required**................._____hrs

3 INITIAL CLIENT MEETING

EXAMPLE

What We Know:
- Review our research about competition
- Review target market profile
- Time needed.................................4 hrs

What We Need:
- Samples of good existing billboard/transit ads
- Time needed.................................2 hrs

**Total Time
Required** ....6 hrs

YOUR HOURS

What You Know:
-
-
- Time needed ...._____hrs

What You Need:
-
- Time needed ...._____hrs

**Total Time
Required**................._____hrs

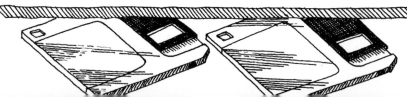

5 CLIENT REQUIREMENTS FOR PROJECT

EXAMPLE

What We Know:

- Budget constraints more important than high quality
- Time needed ....7 hrs

Total Time Required ....7 hrs

YOUR HOURS

What You Know:

-
- Time needed ...._____hrs

Total Time Required ...._____hrs

6 PREPARING COMPS

EXAMPLE

What We Know:

- Scan photos for position on comps
- Full-color computer comps in each sign format
- Mount each sign comp for presentation to client
- Show selected headlines and photographs
- Time needed ....20 hrs

What We Need:

- 10 laser color copies of comps mounted for presentation by client to board of directors
- Time needed ....6 hrs

Total Time Required ....26 hrs

YOUR HOURS

What You Know:

-
-
-
-
- Time needed ...._____hrs

What You Need:

-
- Time needed...................._____hrs

Total Time Required.............._____hrs

TURN PAGE

8 CLIENT MEETINGS

EXAMPLE

What We Know:

- Rough layout approval
- Comp approval
- Mechanical approval
- Time needed ....3 hrs

What We Need:

- Approval/change forms for client signature
- Time needed ....1 hr

Total Time Required...........................4 hrs

YOUR HOURS

What You Know:

-
-
-
- Time needed ...._____hrs

What You Need:

-
- Time needed ...._____hrs

Total Time Required.................._____hrs

7 MECHANICAL PREPARATION

EXAMPLE

What We Know:

- Order type for finished comps
- Prepare boards and overlays for both formats
- Paste-up and proof
- Approve color separation of photos
- Time needed ....7 hrs

What We Need:

- Request bids (prices/schedules) from vendors/subcontractors
- Client approval on mechanicals
- Time needed ....3 hrs

Total Time Required ....10 hrs

YOUR HOURS

What You Know:

-
-
-
- Time needed ...._____hrs

What You Need:

-
- Time needed ...._____hrs

Total Time Required ...._____hrs

WORKSHEET 22 CONTINUED

9 CLERICAL/ADMINISTRATIVE WORK

EXAMPLE

What We Know:
- Prepare price estimate and schedule
- Set up billing account
- Time needed ....1 hr

What We Need:
- Bid confirmation from billboard and transit sign companies
- Time needed ....1 hr

Total Time Required ....2 hrs

YOUR HOURS

What You Know:
-
-
- Time needed ...._____hrs

What You Need:
-
- Time needed ...._____hrs

Total Time Required ...._____hrs

10 TOTAL PROJECT HOURS

EXAMPLE
- Add your hours in Boxes 1-9 to estimate Total Project Hours ....69 hrs
(If you charge different rates for activities, divide the box into sections, one section per rate. For example, if you have the same rate for Comp and for Mechanical Prep, assign one section of the box for those total hours.)

YOUR HOURS
-

12 TIME COSTS

EXAMPLE
- Multiply the total number of project hours in Box 11 by your Hourly Fee Rate to get the Total Project Time Costs $4,560
(To simplify the example, an average hourly fee of $60 has been used. If you charge different rates for activities, multiply the hours for all activities for which you charge the same rate by that rate. Total all the charges. For example, Concept Development + Client Meetings = 70 hrs x $85/hr = $5,950)

YOUR COSTS
-

11 HIDDEN SURPRISE FACTOR

EXAMPLE
- Multiply the amount in Box 10 by .10 (10%); add that to Box 10 to guard against hidden surprises (accidents, emergencies, problems caused by the client, etc.)....................69 + 7 = 76 hrs
(Build a margin into your estimate to avoid cost overruns that anger clients or cost you money. The hidden surprise factor used here is 10% because this client is clearly going to be difficult to work with. It's a good idea to go to 15% on a project you've never done before, but a 5% security blanket may be enough in many cases.)

YOUR HOURS
-

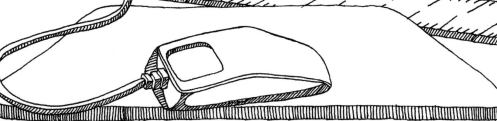

13 URGENCY OF JOB

EXAMPLE

What We Know:
- Deadline is demanding
- Time needed. ....8 hrs
- Rush charge $30/hr

Total Time Required/Total Rush Costs ....8 hrs/$240
- (For a rush project, add your overtime charge or percentage for rush work. Enter here only the cost of the extra charge. For example, at $60, time-and-a-half would cost an extra $30/hour. For 3 hours of overtime, the charge would be $90. If the Total Project Time Cost was $1,200 and your rush charge percentage was 20%, a rush charge on the job would be $240 ($1,200 x .2))

YOUR COSTS

What You Know:
-
- Time needed ...._____hrs
- Rush charge ....$_____/hr

Total Time Required/Total Rush Costs...._____hrs/$_____
-

14 PRODUCTION COSTS

EXAMPLE

What We Know:
- Typesetting $145
- Color separations...............................375
- Supplies...50
- Computer usage..................................150
- Subtotal $720
- Markup (15%) 108

  (Not all artists charge markup; whether you do or don't, be consistent in your practice.)
- Total Known Costs...........................$828

What We Need:
- 10% margin for extra costs................$83

Total Production Costs $911

YOUR COSTS

What You Know:
-
-
-
-
-
-
- Total Known Costs...............$_____

What You Need:
-

Total Production Costs...........................$_____

16 TOTAL PROJECT COSTS

EXAMPLE

What We Know:
- Total Project Costs....................$5,711
- Design to be used only within statewide area for one year..............$0 usage fee

Total Costs.....................$5,711
- (The more rights a client requests, the higher the fee you should charge. Be very careful if a client asks for "all rights" or a "buyout." The fee for the rights involved, if more than one-time rights, must be negotiated with the client and varies from project to project.)
- Sales Tax
  (Calculate sales tax only for the final invoice since it has to be figured on actual costs.)

YOUR COSTS

What You Know:
-
-

Total Costs.................$_____
-

15 PRODUCTION AND FEE COSTS

EXAMPLE
- Add the dollar amounts in Boxes 12, 13 and 14 to get the total amount of service fees and production costs.............$5,711

YOUR COSTS
-

WORKSHEET 23

DIRECT MAIL PACKAGE

Direct mail packages can be simple self-mailers or complex designs involving brochures, promotional letters and return response cards. This example involves a single self-mailer with no return panel.

Accurately estimating the cost of any project involves figuring out the cost of the materials and services you'll purchase on behalf of the client as well as the cost of your time. To arrive at an estimate for a job, fill in the amounts requested as you move through the gameboard. Skip boxes that do not apply, but otherwise go in order until you reach the goal. Inside each box, you'll find an example printed on the left and blank spaces on the right for you to use.

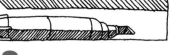

1 PROJECT TITLE— DIRECT MAIL PROMOTIONAL BROCHURE

Client Name: Pleasant Valley Motors
Client Budget: $12,000-15,000
Time Frame: 2 months

2 COMPLEXITY OF JOB

EXAMPLE
What We Know:
- 4-color, 2-fold, 6-panel self-mailer with 10 illustrations of promotional giveaway prizes
- Company history research required
- Target market review desired
- Client has photo references for illustrations
- Time needed ....3 hrs

Total Time
Required...........................3 hrs

YOUR HOURS
What You Know:
-
-
-
- Time needed ...._____hrs

Total Time
Required................._____hrs

4 CONCEPT DEVELOPMENT

EXAMPLE
What We Know:
- Client wants 3 computer-generated layouts
- Design should include sample illustrations and copy
- Time needed ....15 hrs

What We Need:
- Paper samples
- Bulk mailing costs
- Time needed ....2 hrs

Total Time
Required...........................17 hrs

YOUR HOURS
What You Know:
-
-
- Time needed ...._____hrs

What You Need:
-
-
- Time needed....................._____hrs

Total Time
Required.................._____hrs

3 INITIAL CLIENT MEETING

EXAMPLE
What We Know:
- Review client history and market research info
- Bring samples of other direct mail pieces
- Time needed ....2 hrs

What We Need:
- Contract must clearly state kill fee
- Confirm promotion and mailing dates
- Time needed ....1 hr

Total Time
Required...........................3 hrs

YOUR HOURS
What You Know:
-
-
- Time needed ...._____hrs

What You Need:
-
-
- Time needed ...._____hrs

Total Time
Required................._____hrs

5 CLIENT REQUIREMENTS FOR PROJECT

EXAMPLE

What We Know:
- High-end design and paper
- Soft sell desired
- Client easy to work with, open to innovative ideas
- Time needed ....7 hrs

Total Time
Required ....7 hrs

YOUR HOURS

What You Know:
-
-
-
- Time needed ...._____hrs

Total Time
Required ...._____hrs

6 PREPARING COMPS

EXAMPLE

What We Know:
- Fully develop color comp from selected layout
- Final copy revised
- Color illustrations completed
- Time needed ....17 hrs

What We Need:
- Paper sample dummies
- Color copies of brochure comp for sales team review
- Time needed ....3 hrs

Total Time
Required ....20 hrs

YOUR HOURS

What You Know:
-
-
-
- Time needed................._____hrs

What You Need:
-
-
- Time needed ...._____hrs

Total Time
Required ...._____hrs

TURN PAGE

8 CLIENT MEETINGS

EXAMPLE

What We Know:
- Layout, illustration and copy approval
- Comp approval
- Mechanical approval
- Proof approval
- Time needed ....6 hrs

What We Need:
- Approval/change forms for client signature
- Time needed ....1 hr

Total Time
Required ....7 hrs

YOUR HOURS

What You Know:
-
-
-
-
- Time needed ...._____hrs

What You Need:
-
- Time needed ...._____hrs

Total Time
Required ...._____hrs

7 MECHANICAL PREPARATION

EXAMPLE

What We Know:
- Typesetting
- Prepare paste-up, rubys for illustrations, overlays and proofs
- Client approves paste-up and proofs
- Time needed ....10 hrs

What We Need:
- Request bids (prices/schedules) from vendors/subcontractors
- Check color separations
- Time needed ....3 hrs

Total Time
Required ....13 hrs

YOUR HOURS

What You Know:
-
-
-
- Time needed................._____hrs

What You Need:
-
-
- Time needed................._____hrs

Total Time
Required ...._____hrs

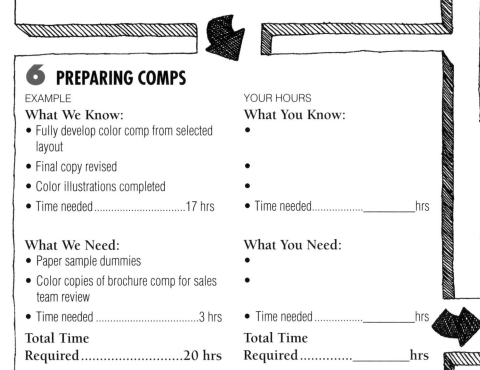

WORSHEET 23 CONTINUED

9 CLERICAL/ADMINISTRATIVE WORK

EXAMPLE

What We Know:
- Prepare price estimate and schedule
- Set up billing account
- Time needed ....1 hr

What We Need:
- Bid confirmation from vendors/subcontractors
- Time needed ....1 hr

Total Time Required ....2 hrs

YOUR HOURS

What You Know:
-
-
- Time needed ...._____hrs

What You Need:
-
- Time needed ...._____hrs

Total Time Required ...._____hrs

10 TOTAL PROJECT HOURS

EXAMPLE
- Add your hours in Boxes 1-9 to estimate Total Project Hours.....................72 hrs
(If you charge different rates for activities, divide the box into sections, one section per rate. For example, if you have the same rate for Comp and for Mechanical Prep, assign one section of the box for those total hours.)

YOUR HOURS
-

12 TIME COSTS

EXAMPLE
- Multiply the total number of project hours in Box 11 by your Hourly Fee Rate to get the Total Project Time Costs.......$4,560
(To simplify the example, an average hourly fee of $60 has been used. If you charge different rates for activities, multiply the hours for all activities for which you charge the same rate by that rate. Total all the charges. For example, Concept Development + Client Meetings = 70 hrs x $85/hr = $5,950)

YOUR COSTS
-

11 HIDDEN SURPRISE FACTOR

EXAMPLE
- Multiply the amount in Box 10 by .05 (5%); add that to Box 10 to guard against hidden surprises (accidents, emergencies, problems caused by the client, etc.) ....72 + 4 = 76 hrs
(Build a margin into your estimate to avoid cost overruns that anger clients or cost you money. The hidden surprise factor used here is 5% because this client is not going to be difficult to work with.)

YOUR HOURS
-

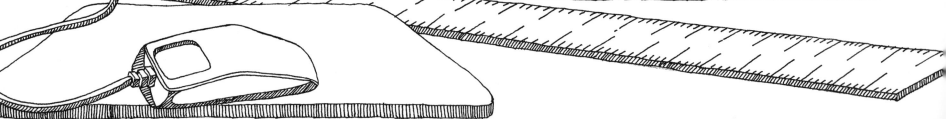

13 URGENCY OF JOB

EXAMPLE

What We Know:
- Deadline is manageable; no overtime
- Time needed ....0 hrs
- Rush charge ....0%/$0

Total Time Required/Total Rush Costs ....0 hrs/$0
- (For a rush project, add your overtime charge or percentage for rush work. Enter here only the cost of the extra charge. For example, at $60, time-and-a-half would cost an extra $30/hour. For 3 hours of overtime, the charge would be $90. If the Total Project Time Cost was $1,200 and your rush charge percentage was 20%, a rush charge on the job would be $240 ($1,200 x .2))

YOUR COSTS

What You Know:
-
- Time needed ...._____hrs
- Rush charge ...._____%/$_____

Total Time Required/Total Rush Costs....._____hrs/$_____
-

16 TOTAL PROJECT COSTS

GOAL

EXAMPLE

What We Know:
- Total Project Costs.....................$13,682
- All rights granted at this price for specified use ....$0 usage fee

Total Costs.....................$13,682
- (The more rights a client requests, the higher the fee you should charge. Be very careful if a client asks for "all rights" or a "buyout." The fee for the rights involved, if more than one-time rights, must be negotiated with the client and varies from project to project.)

- Sales Tax
  (Calculate sales tax only for the final invoice since it has to be figured on actual costs.)

YOUR COSTS

What You Know:
-
-

Total Costs.................$_____
-

14 PRODUCTION COSTS

EXAMPLE

What We Know:
- Typesetting $250
- Computer usage................................250
- Printing...4,000
- Stats..250
- Supplies..55
- Color separations..............................750
- Bulk mail postage 2,000
- Subtotal $7,555
- Markup (15%) 1,133
  (Not all artists charge markup; whether you do or don't, be consistent in your practice.)
- Total Known Costs $8,688

What We Need:
- 5% margin for extra costs................$434

Total Production Costs $9,122

YOUR COSTS

What You Know:
-
-
-
-
-
-
-
-
-
-

- Total Known Costs............$_____

What You Need:
-

Total Production Costs ....$_____

15 PRODUCTION AND FEE COSTS

EXAMPLE
- Total the dollar amounts in Boxes 12, 13 and 14 to get the total amount of service fees and production costs......................................$13,682

YOUR COSTS
-

WORKSHEET 24

EDITORIAL ILLUSTRATION

Prices for editorial illustration are based on flat fees that vary among publications and are usually based on circulation and distribution area. While fees are often much lower here than in advertising, the opportunity provides good visibility and the chance for creative freedom. Expenses are included in the fee, so calculate them and your hours carefully before you accept to ensure the project is profitable.

To arrive at an estimate for an assignment, fill in the amounts requested as you move through the gameboard. Skip boxes that do not apply, but otherwise go in order until you reach the goal. An example has been given for you to follow in coming up with your own figures.

START

1 TYPE OF PROJECT—MAGAZINE COVER ILLUSTRATION

Client Name: Ladies Day Magazine
Type & Size of Client: National consumer magazine
Subject Matter: Motherhood
Style: Detailed rendering
Media: Watercolor and ink
Time: 1-2 weeks

3 INITIAL CLIENT MEETING

EXAMPLE

What I Know:
- Phone meeting
- Discuss impact intended for illustration and audience appeal
- Read article before meeting
- Time needed ....1 hr

What I Need:
- Fax of page layout with vignette showing illustration position
- Copies of 6 recent illustration covers
- Time needed ....1/2 hr

Total Time Required......................1¹/₂ hrs

YOUR HOURS

What You Know:
-
-
-
- Time needed..................._____hrs

What You Need:
-
-
- Time needed..................._____hrs

Total Time Required ...._____hrs

2 COMPLEXITY OF JOB

EXAMPLE

What I Know:
- Highly detailed full-color illustration
- Composition includes 2-3 figures
- Image can be taken from several photographs
- Client supplies reference materials
- Time needed ....1/2 hr

What I Need:
- The article the illustration will flag
- Contract clearly stating kill fee
- Time needed ....1/2 hr

Total Time Required...........................1 hr

YOUR HOURS

What You Know:
-
-
-
-
- Time needed....................._____hrs

What You Need:
-
-
- Time needed.................._____hrs

Total Time Required ...._____hrs

4 CLIENT REQUIREMENTS

EXAMPLE

What I Know:
- Artwork is important showcase piece
- Artwork reproduced by 4-color process
- Client wants 2-3 initial sketches; budget covers only 1 sketch with revisions
- Time needed ....1 hr

What I Need:
- Client agreement to fast turnaround of changes to ensure meeting deadline
- Time needed ....$^{1}\!/_{2}$ hr

Total Time Required ....1$^{1}\!/_{2}$ **hrs**

YOUR HOURS

What You Know:
-
-
-
- Time needed ...._____hrs

What You Need:
-
- Time needed ...._____hrs

Total Time Required............_____**hrs**

TURN PAGE

7 CLIENT MEETINGS

EXAMPLE

What I Know:
- Phone meeting to discuss initial sketch
- Phone meeting to discuss finished art
- Time needed ....1 hr

What I Need:
- Send approval/change form with art for client signature
- Time needed ....$^{1}\!/_{2}$ hr

Total Time Required.......................1$^{1}\!/_{2}$ **hrs**

YOUR HOURS

What You Know:
-
-
- Time needed ...._____hrs

What You Need:
-
- Time needed ...._____hrs

Total Time Required............_____**hrs**

5 DEVELOP SKETCHES

EXAMPLE

What I Know:
- Produce 1 initial color sketch for client review
- Fax sketch to client
- Time needed ....3 hrs

Total Time Required...........................3 **hrs**

YOUR HOURS

What You Know:
-
-
- Time needed ...._____hrs

Total Time Required............_____**hrs**

6 DEVELOP FINISHED ILLUSTRATION

EXAMPLE

What I Know:
- No further sketches needed; minor revisions
- Begin work on finished art using flexible scanner board
- Time needed ....4 hrs

What I Need:
- Have slide made of original for my files
- Time needed ....$^{1}\!/_{2}$ hr

Total Time Required ....4$^{1}\!/_{2}$ **hrs**

YOUR HOURS

What You Know:
-
-
- Time needed ...._____hrs

What You Need:
-
- Time needed ...._____hrs

Total Time Required............_____**hrs**

WORKSHEET 24 CONTINUED

8 PAPERWORK

EXAMPLE

What I Know:
- Prepare estimate of time and materials
- Prepare work schedule
- Set up billing account and prepare invoice
- Time needed ....1½ hrs

**Total Time
Required** ....1½ hrs

YOUR HOURS

What You Know:
-
-
-
- Time needed..............._____hrs

**Total Time
Required** ...._____hrs

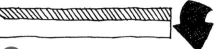

9 TOTAL PROJECT HOURS

EXAMPLE
- Add the hours in Boxes 2-8 to estimate project hours............................14.5 hrs

YOUR HOURS
-

10 HIDDEN SURPRISES

EXAMPLE
- Multiply the amount in Box 9 by .05 (05%) to guard against Hidden Surprises; add that to the amount in Box 9 ....15.5 hrs
  (14.5 x .05 = 1 (.7 rounded up), then 14.5 + 1 = 15.5)

YOUR HOURS
-

(Build a margin into your estimate to avoid cost overruns that anger clients or cost you money.)

12 URGENCY OF JOB

EXAMPLE

What I Know:
- Deadline is manageable
- Time needed ....0 hrs
- Rush charge ....0%/$0

What I Need:
- Is deadline firm?
- Agree that deadline for finished art is 10 days after approval of color copy
- Time needed ....0 hrs/$0
- Rush charge ....0%/$0

**Total Time Required/Total
Rush Costs.................0 hrs/$0**
- (For a rush project, add your usual percentage for overtime or rush work. Most illustrators charge at least time-and-a-half for working around the clock or over a holiday. Adding an additional percentage for overtime to the total is also common; the Total Project Hours would be multiplied by a percentage for the rush charge: 18 hours x $60/hr = $600 + (600 x .05 (5%)) = $630.00 total.)

YOUR COSTS

What You Know:
-
- Time needed ...._____hrs
- Rush charge........_____%/$_____

What You Need:
-
-
- Time needed ...._____hrs/$_____
- Rush charge........_____%/$_____

**Total Time Required/Total
Rush Costs ....____hrs/$____**

11 TIME & WORK FEE

EXAMPLE
- Multiply the total hours by your hourly rate (15.5 hrs x $60)...............$3,700

YOUR COSTS
-

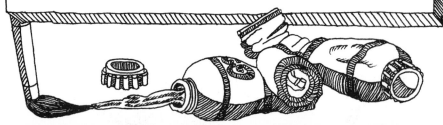

13 EXPENSES

EXAMPLE

What I Know:
- Color photocopy $8
- Special watercolor paper 10
- Fax/overnight mail. 43
- Subtotal $61
- Markup (0%) 0
  (Because expenses are included in the flat fee, you don't need to figure a markup. Simply allow a margin for extra costs. Not all artists charge markup; whether you do or don't, be consistent in your practice.)

Total $61

What I Need:
- Margin for Extra Costs (10%) $6.10
  (61 x .10 = $6.10)
  (Because this assignment is on a flat fee basis, you want to budget a margin for extra costs to make sure even unanticipated expenses are covered before you sign the agreement. Because the costs here are so low, a margin of 10% is used for safety.)

Total Expenses $67.10

YOUR COSTS

What You Know:
-
-
-
-
-

Total ....$_____

What You Need:
-

Total Expenses ...$_____

15 TOTAL PROJECT COSTS

EXAMPLE
- Total Boxes 11, 12, 13 and 14 and then round up to the nearest fifth or tenth dollar $1,199.10
- Sales Tax
  (Calculate sales tax only for the final invoice since it has to be figured on actual costs.)

YOUR COSTS
-

-

14 RIGHTS SOLD

EXAMPLE

What I Know:
- One-time North American magazine rights for Ladies Day
- Ladies Day is a national consumer magazine
- Client wants 3 months' exclusivity
- If artwork is used for other purposes, additional fee will be negotiated
- Original art will be returned to me
- Get written agreement spelling out rights being purchased

Usage Fee $202
- (Since this is a flat fee agreement, an initial, separate usage fee wouldn't be charged. After costs, this is what you're being paid for usage on this assignment.)

YOUR COSTS

What You Know:
-
-
-
-
-

Usage Fee ....$_____
-

GOAL

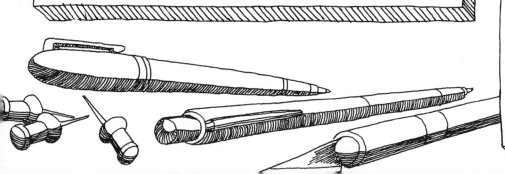

WORKSHEET 25

ANNUAL REPORT ILLUSTRATIONS

This is an example of pricing illustrations for an annual report. Prices here are based on an hourly rate, although sometimes flat fees are offered. Be certain to accurately estimate your hours so your client has a fair idea of your fee. Since expenses will be high on this type of job, you can also add a markup to them; expenses will be billed separately from the illustration fee.

To arrive at an estimate for an assignment, fill in the amounts requested as you move through the gameboard. Skip boxes that do not apply, but otherwise go in order until you reach the goal. An example has been given for you to follow in coming up with your own figures.

START

1 TYPE OF PROJECT—ANNUAL REPORT ILLUSTRATIONS

Client Name: **Techtronics Corporation**
Type & Size of Client: **Midsized manufacturer of CD components**
Subject Matter: **CD components in a variety of home interior settings**
Style: **Tightly rendered pen & ink drawings**
Medium: **Pen & ink**
Time: **3 months**
Budget: **$5,000-7,000**

3 INITIAL CLIENT MEETING

EXAMPLE	YOUR HOURS
What I Know:	**What You Know:**
• Discuss audience and slant for drawings	•
• Show examples of my work that was done in the style client favors	•
• Be sure I understand what client wants	•
• Time needed..................................2 hrs	• Time needed ...._____hrs
What I Need:	**What You Need:**
• Contract clearly stating kill fee and usage agreement	•
• Past issues of the company's annuals	•
• Time needed ....1 hr	• Time needed.................._____hrs
Total Time	**Total Time**
Required ....3 hrs	Required ...._____hrs

2 COMPLEXITY OF JOB

EXAMPLE	YOUR HOURS
What I Know:	**What You Know:**
• 3 half-page, b&w illustrations, 4 spot illustrations	•
• Client will provide reference photos	•
• Pen & ink detailed crosshatch drawings	•
• Time needed ....5 hrs	• Time needed ...._____hrs
What I Need:	**What You Need:**
• Collect magazine photographs of home interiors	•
• Time needed ....5 hrs	• Time needed.................._____hrs
Total Time	**Total Time**
Required.........................10 hrs	Required................._____hrs

4 CLIENT REQUIREMENTS

TURN PAGE

EXAMPLE

What I Know:
- High-end, glossy production
- 2 spot drawings will be screened back to 30% so type can surprint
- Time needed ....3 hrs

What I Need:
- Tissues of page layouts for illustration sizing
- Time needed ....1 hr

Total Time Required...............................4 hrs

YOUR HOURS

What You Know:
-
-
- Time needed ...._____hrs

What You Need:
-
- Time needed ...._____hrs

Total Time Required............_____hrs

---

5 DEVELOP SKETCHES

EXAMPLE

What I Know:
- Client wants pencil sketches of illustrations before I begin final drawings
- Allow time for revisions, second review and final approval
- Time needed ....15 hrs

What I Need:
- Copies of sketches for client to present to board of directors
- Time needed ....1 hr

Total Time Required...............................16 hrs

YOUR HOURS

What You Know:
-
-
- Time needed ...._____hrs

What You Need:
-
- Time needed....................._____hrs

Total Time Required............_____hrs

---

7 CLIENT MEETINGS

EXAMPLE

What I Know:
- Approval of rough sketches
- Approval of finished drawings
- Time needed ....5 hrs

What I Need:
- Approval/change forms for client signature
- Time needed ....5 hrs

Total Time Required ....10 hrs

YOUR HOURS

What You Know:
-
-
- Time needed ...._____hrs

What You Need:
-
- Time needed ...._____hrs

Total Time Required............_____hrs

---

6 DEVELOP FINISHED ILLUSTRATION

EXAMPLE

What I Know:
- Finish drawings
- Get client approval of drawings
- Time needed ....25 hrs

What I Need:
- Stats of all drawings
- Time needed ....2 hrs

Total Time Required ....27 hrs

YOUR HOURS

What You Know:
-
-
- Time needed ...._____hrs

What You Need:
-
- Time needed ...._____hrs

Total Time Required............_____hrs

WORSHEET 25 *CONTINUED*

8 PAPERWORK

EXAMPLE

What I Know:
- Prepare price quote
- Prepare work schedule
- Prepare invoice
- Time needed ....4 hrs

What I Need:
- Negotiate with client the expenses that will be billed separately
- Time needed ....1 hr

Total Time Required............................**5 hrs**

YOUR HOURS

What You Know:
-
-
-
- Time needed..............._____hrs

What You Need:
-
- Time needed ...._____hrs

Total Time Required ...._____**hrs**

9 TOTAL PROJECT HOURS

EXAMPLE
- Add the hours in 2-8 to estimate project hours ....75 hrs

YOUR HOURS
-

10 HIDDEN SURPRISES

EXAMPLE
- Multiply the amount in Box 9 by .15 (15%) to guard against Hidden Surprises; add that to the amount in Box 9 ....86.25 hrs
  (75 x .15 = 11.25, then 75 + 11.25 = 86.25)
  (Build a margin into your estimate to avoid cost overruns that anger clients or cost you money.)

YOUR HOURS
-

12 URGENCY OF JOB

EXAMPLE

What I Know:
- Time frame is adequate if there are 1 or 2 revisions
- Time needed ....0 hrs
- Rush charge ....0%/$0

What I Need:
- A written agreement with client specifying that after 2 revisions extra charges will be billed
- Time needed ....0 hrs/$0
- Rush charge ....0%/$0

Total Time Required/Total Rush Costs.................**0 hrs/$0**
- (For a rush project, add your usual percentage for overtime or rush work. Most illustrators charge at least time-and-a-half for working around the clock or over a holiday. Adding an additional percentage for overtime to the total is also common; the Total Project Hours would be multiplied by a percentage for the rush charge: 10 hours x $60/hr = $600 + (600 x .05 (5%)) = $630.00 total.)

YOUR COSTS

What You Know:
-
- Time needed ...._____hrs
- Rush charge......._____%/$_____

What You Need:
-
- Time needed ...._____hrs/$_____
- Rush charge......._____%/$_____

Total Time Required/Total Rush Costs ..._____hrs/$_____
-

11 TIME & WORK FEE

EXAMPLE
- Multiply the total hours by your hourly rate (86.25 hrs x $60) $5,175

YOUR COSTS
-

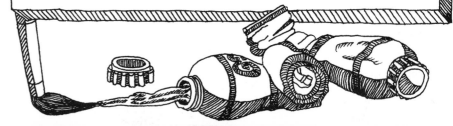

13 EXPENSES

EXAMPLE

What I Know:
- Stats..................................$200
- Supplies.............................50
- Subtotal $250
- Markup (20%) 50
  (A 20% markup is added because expenses are less than $1,000. Not all artists charge markup; whether you do or don't, be consistent in your practice.)

Total $300

What I Need:
- Margin for Extra Costs (10%) $30
  ($300 x .10 (10%) = $30)
  (Expenses here are billed separately from the fee. Always try to negotiate that expenses be paid separately in case unexpected expenses arise. Whenever an unexpected expense is incurred, notify the client immediately. If a client doesn't sign off on the expense at the time it's incurred, he may refuse to pay it on your invoice or above the flat fee.)

Total Expenses....................$330

YOUR COSTS

What You Know:
-
-
-
-

Total ....$_____

What You Need:
-

Total Expenses ...$_____

15 TOTAL PROJECT COSTS

EXAMPLE
- Total Boxes 11, 12, 13 and 14 and then round up to the nearest fifth or tenth dollar $6,005
- Sales Tax
  (Calculate sales tax only for the final invoice since it has to be figured on actual costs.)

YOUR COSTS
-

-

14 RIGHTS SOLD

EXAMPLE

What I Know:
- One-time use only. If design is to be used for other purposes, the price will be renegotiated.
- I retain ownership of original art.

Usage Fee $500

YOUR COSTS

What You Know:
-

-

Usage Fee ....$_____

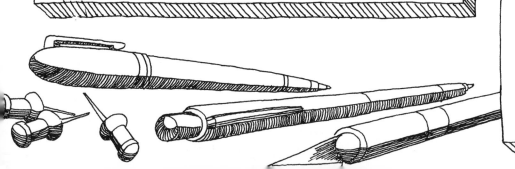

WORKSHEET 26

BOOK COVER ILLUSTRATION

This example demonstrates how to figure costs for a paperback book cover illustration. In this case, the client pays a flat fee and supplies a sketch prepared by the book cover's designer. Most publishing companies pay flat fees; royalties may be offered in some situations. Expenses are included in this flat fee project.

To arrive at an estimate for an assignment, fill in the amounts requested as you move through the gameboard. Skip boxes that do not apply, but otherwise go in order until you reach the goal. An example has been given for you to follow in coming up with your own figures.

START

1 TYPE OF PROJECT— BOOK COVER ILLUSTRATION

Client Name: Farber Publishing Company
Type & Size of Client: Midsized publishing company releasing 40 mass market paperbacks, trade hardcover and paperbacks per year
Subject Matter: Adult contemporary fiction
Style: Full-color, photo-realistic
Medium: Colored pencil and graphite
Time: 1 month
Budget: $2,500

3 INITIAL CLIENT MEETING

EXAMPLE

What I Know:
- Review covers of publisher's other mass market titles
- Discuss manuscript and review designer's concept
- Agree that I can submit compatible ideas
- Time needed..................................8 hrs

What I Need:
- Copy of layout and designer's sketch
- Contract clearly stating kill fee
- Time needed ....1 hr

Total Time
Required ....9 hrs

YOUR HOURS

What You Know:
-
-
-
- Time needed ...._____hrs

What You Need:
-
-
- Time needed...................._____hrs

Total Time
Required ...._____hrs

2 COMPLEXITY OF JOB

EXAMPLE

What I Know:
- The cover layout has been approved by the publisher
- Designer provided a concept sketch of the illustration
- Time needed..................................1 hr

What I Need:
- To read the manuscript
- Copies of other cover illustrations on similar titles
- Time needed..................................1 hr

Total Time
Required ....2 hrs

YOUR HOURS

What You Know:
-
-
- Time needed ...._____hrs

What You Need:
-
-
- Time needed..................._____hrs

Total Time
Required ...._____hrs

4 CLIENT REQUIREMENTS

TURN PAGE

EXAMPLE

What I Know:
- Client will handle color separation
- Illustration must recreate a specific scene in the book
- Client wants a romantic, soft look with photo-realistic imagery
- Time needed ....2 hrs

What I Need:
- Client's agreement to timely approval to allow adequate time for revision and completion
- Time needed ....1 hr

**Total Time
Required** ....3 hrs

YOUR HOURS

What You Know:
-
-
-
- Time needed ...._____hrs

What You Need:
-
- Time needed ...._____hrs

**Total Time
Required** ...._____hrs

7 CLIENT MEETINGS

EXAMPLE

What I Know:
- Phone meeting to discuss revisions to finished illustration
- Written approval of finished illustration
- Ship final illustration overnight
- Time needed ....1 hr

What I Need:
- Contract and approval/change forms for client signature
- Time needed ....1 hr

**Total Time
Required** ....2 hrs

YOUR HOURS

What You Know:
-
-
-
- Time needed ...._____hrs

What You Need:
-
- Time needed ...._____hrs

**Total Time
Required** ...._____hrs

5 DEVELOP SKETCHES

EXAMPLE

What I Know:
- 2 rough, color tissue sketches, to size
- Sketches of my original concepts
- C-prints of sketches sent overnight for approval
- Time needed ....5 hrs

What I Need:
- Phone meeting with client to discuss tissue sketches
- Time needed ....1 hr

**Total Time
Required** ....6 hrs

YOUR HOURS

What You Know:
-
-
-
- Time needed ...._____hrs

What You Need:
-
- Time needed................_____hrs

**Total Time
Required** ...._____hrs

6 DEVELOP FINISHED ILLUSTRATION

EXAMPLE

What I Know:
- Complete finished illustration of selected sketch
- Make client's revisions
- Time needed ....6 hrs

What I Need:
- Send original overnight to client; keep color copy for my files
- Time needed ....1 hr

**Total Time
Required** ....7 hrs

YOUR HOURS

What You Know:
-
-
- Time needed ...._____hrs

What You Need:
-
- Time needed ...._____hrs

**Total Time
Required** ...._____hrs

WORKSHEET 26 *CONTINUED*

8 PAPERWORK

EXAMPLE

What I Know:
- Prepare rights agreement for inclusion in contract
- Prepare work schedule
- Prepare invoice
- Time needed ....2 hrs

What I Need:
- Be sure that the budget is sufficient to cover my time
- Time needed ....1 hr

Total Time Required............................3 hrs

YOUR HOURS

What You Know:
-
-
-
- Time needed................_____hrs

What You Need:
-
- Time needed...................._____hrs

Total Time Required ...._____hrs

9 TOTAL PROJECT HOURS

EXAMPLE
- Total the hours in Boxes 2-8 to estimate number of project hours ....32 hrs

YOUR HOURS
-

10 HIDDEN SURPRISES

EXAMPLE
- Multiply the amount in Box 9 by .10 (10%) to guard against Hidden Surprises; add that to the amount in Box 9 ....35 hrs
  (32 x .10 = 3, then 32 + 3 = 35)
  (Build a margin into your estimate to avoid cost overruns that anger clients or cost you money.)

YOUR HOURS
-

12 URGENCY OF JOB

EXAMPLE

What I Know:
- Time frame is manageable
- Time needed ....0 hrs
- Rush charge ....0%/$0

What I Need:
- Be sure that client will approve sketches and revisions in a timely manner, so no overtime or rush charges are needed
- Time needed ....0 hrs/$0
- Rush charge ....0%/$0

Total Time Required/Total Rush Costs.................0 hrs/$0
- (For a rush project, add your usual percentage for overtime or rush work. Most illustrators charge at least time-and-a-half for working around the clock or over a holiday. Adding an additional percentage for overtime to the total is also common; the Total Project Hours would be multiplied by a percentage for the rush charge: 10 hours x $60/hr = $600 + (600 x .05 (5%)) = $630.00 total.)

YOUR COSTS

What You Know:
-
- Time needed ...._____hrs
- Rush charge......._____%/$_____

What You Need:
-
- Time needed ...._____hrs/$_____
- Rush charge......._____%/$_____

Total Time Required/Total Rush Costs ...._____hrs/$_____
-

11 TIME & WORK FEE

EXAMPLE
- Multiply the total hours by your hourly rate (35 hours x $60) $2,100

YOUR COSTS
-

13 EXPENSES

EXAMPLE	YOUR COSTS
What I Know:	**What You Know:**

What I Know:
- Postage.................................$36
- C-prints 15
- Supplies...................................50
- Subtotal $101
- Markup (20%) 20
  (A 20% markup was added because expenses are less than $1,000. Not all artists charge markup; whether you do or don't, be consistent in your practice.)

Total $121

What I Need:
- Margin for Extra Costs (10%) $12.00
  (121 x .10 = $12.00)
  (Because this assignment is on a flat fee basis, you want to budget a margin for extra costs to make sure even unanticipated expenses are covered before you sign the agreement. Because the costs here are so low, a margin of 10% is used for safety. Expenses are not billed separately from the fee. You should, though, always try to negotiate separate billing, in case unexpected expenses arise. Whenever additional expenses are incurred, notify the client immediately. If a client doesn't sign off on the expense at that time, he may refuse to pay it on your invoice.)

Total Expenses $133.00

What You Know:
-
-
-
-
-

Total ....$_____

What You Need:
-

Total Expenses ....$_____

15 TOTAL PROJECT COSTS

EXAMPLE	YOUR COSTS

- Total Boxes 11, 12, 13 and 14 and then round up to the nearest fifth or tenth dollar $2,500
- Sales Tax
  (Calculate sales tax only for the final invoice since it has to be figured on actual costs.)

YOUR COSTS
-
-

GOAL

14 RIGHTS SOLD

EXAMPLE	YOUR COSTS
What I Know:	**What You Know:**

What I Know:
- First reproduction rights only at the agreed to price
- If artwork is to be used for other than its original purpose, the price must be renegotiated
- Original artwork will be returned to the artist

Usage Fee $267
- (Since this is a flat fee agreement, an initial, separate usage fee wouldn't be charged. After costs, this is what you're being paid for usage on this assignment.)

What You Know:
-
-
-

Usage Fee ....$_____
-

WORKSHEET 27

BOOK INTERIOR ILLUSTRATION

Prices for book illustration are based on either a flat fee or an advance against royalties; the arrangement depends on how important the art is. This worksheet involves a flat fee since the illustrations for the novel are secondary to the text. Be sure to figure your costs accurately, so the fee covers your time and expenses, which are included in the fee.

To arrive at an estimate for an assignment, fill in the amounts requested as you move through the gameboard. Skip boxes that do not apply, but otherwise go in order until you reach the goal. An example has been given for you to follow in coming up with your own figures.

START

1 TYPE OF PROJECT—ILLUSTRATIONS FOR A NOVEL

Client Name: Youth Press
Type & Size of Client: Small publisher of young adult fiction
Subject Matter: Mystery story involving 2 children and a dog
Style: Realistic
Medium: Pencil
Time: 3 months
Fee: $4,500

3 INITIAL CLIENT MEETING

EXAMPLE
What I Know:
- Phone meeting
- Determine exactly what client wants in illustrations
- Confirm fee and deadlines
- Time needed ....½ hr

What I Need:
- Page layouts showing text placement and illustration size
- Copy of manuscript
- Samples of similar illustrations used by publisher
- Time needed ....3½ hrs

**Total Time
Required** ....4 hrs

YOUR HOURS
What You Know:
-
-
-
- Time needed ...._____hrs

What You Need:
-
-
-
- Time needed ...._____hrs

**Total Time
Required**..............._____hrs

2 COMPLEXITY OF JOB

EXAMPLE
What I Know:
- B&W halftone illustrations: 1 full spread, 3 full pages, 2 half pages, 6 quarter pages
- Requires fax transmissions, overnight mailings and long distance charges
- Time needed ....3 hrs

What I Need:
- Find children/dog reference photos
- Contract clearly stating kill fee and rights sold
- Time needed ....1 hr

**Total Time
Required**..........................4 hrs

YOUR HOURS
What You Know:
-
-
- Time needed ...._____hrs

What You Need:
-
-
- Time needed.................._____hrs

**Total Time
Required** ...._____hrs

4 CLIENT REQUIREMENTS

EXAMPLE

What I Know:
- Client wants 2 rough idea sketches for each illustration; 24 sketches total
- Time needed ....4½ hrs

What I Need:
- Negotiate time for revisions
- Time needed....................................½ hr

Total Time Required............................5 hrs

YOUR HOURS

What You Know:
-
- Time needed ...._____hrs

What You Need:
-
- Time needed ...._____hrs

Total Time Required............_____hrs

TURN PAGE

7 CLIENT MEETINGS

EXAMPLE

What I Know:
- Phone meeting to discuss initial sketches
- Phone meeting to discuss finished illustrations
- Mail finished artwork
- Send approval/change form with each stage of artwork
- Time needed ....1 hr

What I Need:
- Build in time for additional reviews
- Time needed ....1 hr

Total Time Required ....2 hrs

YOUR HOURS

What You Know:
-
-
-
-
- Time needed ...._____hrs

What You Need:
-
- Time needed ...._____hrs

Total Time Required............_____hrs

5 DEVELOP SKETCHES

EXAMPLE

What I Know:
- Produce idea pencil sketches for client approval
- Overnight mail of sketches to client
- Client will fax sketches back with revisions
- Time needed ....15 hrs

What I Need:
- A phone meeting with client to discuss sketches, selection and revisions
- Time needed ....1 hr

Total Time Required............................16 hrs

YOUR HOURS

What You Know:
-
-
-
- Time needed ...._____hrs

What You Need:
-
- Time needed................_____hrs

Total Time Required............_____hrs

6 DEVELOP FINISHED ILLUSTRATION

EXAMPLE

What I Know:
- Send photocopies of finished work for client approval or revisions
- Keep halftones of each illustration for my files
- Time needed ....20 hrs

What I Need:
- Send originals to client
- Time needed ....8 hrs

Total Time Required ....28 hrs

YOUR HOURS

What You Know:
-
-
- Time needed ...._____hrs

What You Need:
-
- Time needed ...._____hrs

Total Time Required............_____hrs

WORKSHEET 27 *CONTINUED*

8 PAPERWORK

EXAMPLE

What I Know:
- Prepare an estimate of my time and costs
- Prepare work schedule
- Prepare contract
- Prepare invoice
- Time needed ....3 hrs

What I Need:
- Client's budget
- Discuss if expenses are part of fee
- Time needed.....................................½ hr

Total Time Required.........................3½ hrs

YOUR HOURS

What You Know:
-
-
-
-
- Time needed..............._____hrs

What You Need:
-
-
- Time needed................._____hrs

Total Time Required ...._____hrs

9 TOTAL PROJECT HOURS

EXAMPLE
- Total the hours in Boxes 2-8 to estimate number of project hours ....62.5 hrs

YOUR HOURS
-

10 HIDDEN SURPRISES

EXAMPLE
- Multiply the amount in Box 9 by .10 (10%) to guard against Hidden Surprises and add that to the amount in Box 9 ....68.5 hrs
  (62.5 x .10 = 6, then 62.5 + 6 = 68.5)
  (Build a margin into your estimate to avoid cost overruns that anger clients or cost you money.)

YOUR HOURS
-

12 URGENCY OF JOB

EXAMPLE

What I Know:
- Deadline is manageable
- Time needed ....0 hrs
- Rush charge ....0%/$0

What I Need:
- To agree with client that only 2 rounds of revisions are included in this fee
- Time needed ....0 hrs/$0
- Rush charge ....0%/$0

Total Time Required/Total Rush Costs.................0 hrs/$0
- (For a rush project, add your usual percentage for overtime or rush work. Most illustrators charge at least time-and-a-half for working around the clock or over a holiday. Adding an additional percentage for overtime to the total is also common; the Total Project Hours would be multiplied by a percentage for the rush charge: 10 hours x $60/hr = $600 + (600 x .05 (5%)) = $630.00 total.)

YOUR COSTS

What You Know:
-
- Time needed ...._____hrs
- Rush charge........_____%/$_____

What You Need:
-
- Time needed ...._____hrs/$_____
- Rush charge........_____%/$_____

Total Time Required/Total Rush Costs ...._____hrs/$_____
-

11 TIME & WORK FEE

EXAMPLE
- Multiply the total hours by your hourly rate (68.5 hrs x $60) $4,110

YOUR COSTS
-

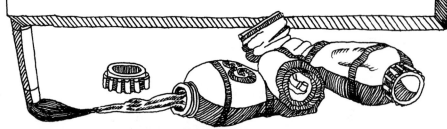

13 EXPENSES

EXAMPLE
What I Know:
- Halftones $100
- Telephone, postage and faxes 85
- Subtotal $185
- Markup (0%) 0
  (Because expenses are included in the flat fee, you don't need to figure a markup. Simply allow a margin for extra costs. Not all artists charge markup; whether you do or don't, be consistent in your practice.)

Total $185

What I Need:
- Margin for Extra Costs (10%) $18.50
  (185 x .10 = $18.50)
  (Because this assignment is on a flat fee basis, you want to budget a margin for extra costs to make sure even unanticipated expenses are covered before you sign the agreement. Because the costs here are so low, a margin of 10% is used for safety. For this project, expenses are not billed separately from the flat fee. You should, though, always try to negotiate separate billing in case unexpected expenses arise.)

Total Expenses $203.50

YOUR COSTS
What You Know:
-
-
-
-

Total ....$_____

What You Need:
-

Total Expenses ...$_____

15 TOTAL PROJECT COSTS

EXAMPLE
- Total Boxes 11, 12, 13 and 14 and then round up to the nearest fifth or tenth dollar $4,500
- Sales Tax
  (Calculate sales tax only for the final invoice since it has to be figured on actual costs.)

YOUR COSTS
-

-

GOAL

14 RIGHTS SOLD

EXAMPLE
What I Know:
- First reproduction rights only at the agreed to price
- If artwork is to be used for other than its original purpose, the price must be renegotiated
- Original artwork will be returned to the artist

Usage Fee $186.50
- (Since this is a flat fee agreement, an initial, separate usage fee wouldn't be charged. After costs, this is what you're being paid for usage on this assignment.)

YOUR COSTS
What You Know:
-

-

-

Usage Fee ....$_____
-

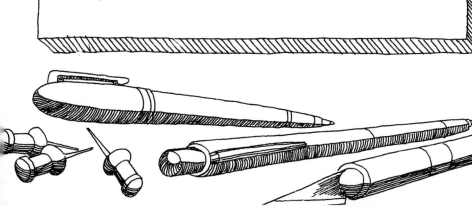

WORKSHEET 28

MEDICAL ILLUSTRATION

This example shows how to price medical illustrations for a textbook, where fees are usually much lower than in advertising. Fees for editorial medical illustrations in consumer health and science publications are higher than those used in medical journals or textbooks. Fees are also based on the complexity of the work, the research involved, usage and the artist's reputation. Expenses are billed separately from the fee.

To arrive at an estimate for an assignment, fill in the amounts requested as you move through the gameboard. Skip boxes that do not apply, but otherwise go in order until you reach the goal. An example has been given for you to follow in coming up with your own figures.

START

1 TYPE OF PROJECT—MEDICAL TEXTBOOK ILLUSTRATIONS

Client Name: MedCom Textbook Company
Type & Size of Client: Midsize, specialty publisher
Subject Matter: The effects of illness or injury to the spine
Style: Photo-realistic
Medium: Pen & ink, full-color airbrush
Time: 5 months
Budget: $9,000-11,000

3 INITIAL CLIENT MEETING

EXAMPLE

What I Know:
- Client will supply some reference materials and list of specialists I can contact
- Phone meeting to discuss deadlines, budget, usage and drawings
- Time needed..................................3 hrs

What I Need:
- Client's other illustrated textbooks
- Client's concept sketches, color palette and page layouts
- Time needed................................2 hrs

Total Time
Required ....5 hrs

YOUR HOURS

What You Know:
-
-
- Time needed ...._____hrs

What You Need:
-
-
- Time needed...................._____hrs

Total Time
Required ...._____hrs

2 COMPLEXITY OF JOB

EXAMPLE

What I Know:
- 5 b&w line drawings (¼ to ½ page); 10 detailed b&w airbrush renderings (⅓ to ½ page); 7 detailed full-color airbrush diagrams (½ to full page)
- Artwork floats on white background
- Time needed ....4 hrs

What I Need:
- Visual references for research
- Drawings reviewed by panel of doctors
- Time needed ....4 hrs

Total Time
Required ....8 hrs

YOUR HOURS

What You Know:
-
-
- Time needed ...._____hrs

What You Need:
-
-
- Time needed...................._____hrs

Total Time
Required ...._____hrs

4 CLIENT REQUIREMENTS

What I Know:
- Client is demanding and prone to making last-minute changes
- Client wants tissue overlays showing placement of labels
- Must be finely rendered illustrations
- Time needed ....9 hrs

What I Need:
- To know client's approval process and requirements for presenting and delivering artwork
- Written agreement limiting the number of revisions
- Time needed ....3 hrs

Total Time Required..........................12 hrs

YOUR HOURS

What You Know:
-
-
-
- Time needed ...._____hrs

What You Need:
-
-
- Time needed ...._____hrs

Total Time Required............_____hrs

TURN PAGE

7 CLIENT MEETINGS

EXAMPLE

What I Know:
- Phone meeting to discuss roughs
- Phone meeting to discuss revisions
- Phone meeting to discuss artwork
- Send approval/change forms with each stage of artwork
- Deliver finished art
- Time needed ....3 hrs

What I Need:
- Build in margin for at least two additional approval meetings
- Time needed ....5 hrs

Total Time Required ....8 hrs

YOUR HOURS

What You Know:
-
-
-
-
-
- Time needed................_____hrs

What You Need:
-
- Time needed................_____hrs

Total Time Required ...._____hrs

5 DEVELOP SKETCHES

EXAMPLE

What I Know:
- Client wants 1 rough pencil sketch per illustration
- Indicate colors on roughs
- Send sketches overnight for client/panel review
- Time needed ....25 hrs

What I Need:
- Time for revisions before final work begins
- Send revisions overnight to client for approval
- Time needed ....15 hrs

Total Time Required..........................40 hrs

YOUR HOURS

What You Know:
-
-
-
- Time needed ...._____hrs

What You Need:
-
-
- Time needed ...._____hrs

Total Time Required............_____hrs

6 DEVELOP FINISHED ILLUSTRATION

EXAMPLE

What I Know:
- Complete all 22 pieces on flexible board
- Send originals overnight to client
- Time needed...............................60 hrs

What I Need:
- Have slides taken of each piece for my files
- Time needed................................3 hrs

Total Time Required ....63 hrs

YOUR HOURS

What You Know:
-
-
- Time needed ...._____hrs

What You Need:
-
- Time needed ...._____hrs

Total Time Required............._____hrs

WORKSHEET 28 *CONTINUED*

8 PAPERWORK

EXAMPLE

What I Know:
- Prepare estimate of my fee
- Develop work schedule
- Prepare invoice
- Document research time and references
- Time needed ....5 hrs

What I Need:
- Discuss if expenses are part of fee
- Client's budget
- Time needed ....1 hr

Total Time Required ....6 hrs

YOUR HOURS

What You Know:
-
-
-
-
- Time needed..............._____hrs

What You Need:
-
-
- Time needed..............._____hrs

Total Time Required ...._____hrs

9 TOTAL PROJECT HOURS

EXAMPLE
- Total the hours in Boxes 2-8 to estimate number of project hours ....142 hrs

YOUR HOURS
-

10 HIDDEN SURPRISES

EXAMPLE
- Multiply the amount in Box 9 by .15 (15%) to guard against Hidden Surprises and add that to the amount in Box 9 ....163 hrs
(142 x .15 = 21, then 142 + 21 = 163) (Build a margin into your estimate to avoid cost overruns that anger clients or cost you money.)

YOUR HOURS
-

12 URGENCY OF JOB

EXAMPLE

What I Know:
- Deadline is manageable if number of revisions are limited
- Time needed ....0 hrs
- Rush charge ....0%/$0

What I Need:
- Be sure that written agreement is enforced regarding the number of revisions so I stay within money and time budget
- Time needed ....0 hrs/$0
- Rush charge ....0%/$0

Total Time Required/Total Rush Costs.................0 hrs/$0
- (For a rush project, add your usual percentage for overtime or rush work. Most illustrators charge at least time-and-a-half for working around the clock or over a holiday. Adding an additional percentage for overtime to the total is also common; the Total Project Hours would be multiplied by a percentage for the rush charge: 10 hours x $60/hr = $600 + (600 x .05 (5%)) = $630.00 total.)

YOUR COSTS

What You Know:
-
- Time needed................._____hrs
- Rush charge......._____%/$_____

What You Need:
-
- Time needed........._____hrs/$_____
- Rush charge......._____%/$_____

Total Time Required/Total Rush Costs ..._____hrs/$_____
-

11 TIME & WORK FEE

EXAMPLE
- Multiply the total hours by your hourly rate (163 hrs x $60) $9,780

YOUR COSTS
-

13 EXPENSES

EXAMPLE

What I Know:
- Postage..............................$54
- Stats.......................................20
- Color slides 70
- Subtotal $144
- Markup (20%) 29
  (Some artists charge a markup of 20-25% on expenses under $1,000 and 15% on expenses over $1,000. Whether you do or don't charge a markup, be consistent in your practice.)

Total $173

What I Need:
- Margin for Extra Costs (20%) $35
  ($173 x .20 = $35)
- Get written agreement that expenses are billed separately.
  (Expenses here are billed separately from the fee. Always try to negotiate this arrangement in case unexpected expenses arise. Whenever additional expenses are incurred, notify the client immediately. If a client doesn't sign off on the expense at the time it's incurred, he may refuse to pay it on your invoice.)

Total Expenses.....................$208

YOUR COSTS

What You Know:
-
-
-
-
-

Total ....$_____

What You Need:
-
-

Total Expenses ...$_____

15 TOTAL PROJECT COSTS

EXAMPLE
- Total Boxes 11, 12, 13 and 14 and then round up to the nearest fifth or tenth dollar $10,488
- Sales Tax
  (Calculate sales tax only for the final invoice since it has to be figured on actual costs.)

YOUR COSTS
-
-

GOAL

14 RIGHTS SOLD

EXAMPLE

What I Know:
- Client wants exclusive, world textbook rights for this hardcover edition
- I can sell illustrations to magazines and medical journals
- Original artwork will be returned
- If the artwork is to be used in a second edition of the hardcover textbook or in a paperback edition, an additional fee will be negotiated

Usage Fee $500

YOUR COSTS

What You Know:
-
-
-

Usage Fee ....$_____

WORKSHEET 29

ARCHITECTURAL ILLUSTRATION

Pricing architectural renderings for both interior and exterior views is based on the amount of detailing, the number of buildings or interior scenes, and the total number of views. Separate billing of expenses is agreed to in writing; expenses usually include production charges, travel expenses and hiring a consultant, if necessary. In addition, reproduction rights must be clearly specified and agreed to in writing.

To arrive at an estimate for an assignment, fill in the amounts requested as you move through the gameboard. Skip boxes that do not apply, but otherwise go in order until you reach the goal. An example has been given for you to follow in coming up with your own figures.

START

1 TYPE OF PROJECT—ARCHITECTURAL ILLUSTRATION

Client Name: **Davis & Jenkins, Architects**
Type & Size of Client: **Local, midsized architectural firm**
Subject Matter: **Group of 3 buildings in cancer treatment center**
Style: **Photo-realistic, highly complex and detailed**
Medium: **Watercolor**
Time: **1 week**
Budget: **$3,500-4,500**

3 INITIAL CLIENT MEETING

EXAMPLE

What I Know:
- Review client sketches; tour & photograph construction sites
- Review plans
- Discuss options for perspective and angle of view
- Time needed ....3 hrs

What I Need:
- Detailed plans and elevations
- A copy of the plans on computer disk, if available
- Time needed ....1 hr

Total Time
Required ....4 hrs

YOUR HOURS

What You Know:
-
-
-
- Time needed ...._____hrs

What You Need:
-
-
- Time needed ...._____hrs

Total Time
Required ...._____hrs

2 COMPLEXITY OF JOB

EXAMPLE

What I Know:
- Requires overtime
- Will be used in fund-raising brochure
- Involves a highly detailed, large-scale watercolor rendering of 3 building exteriors and environmental surroundings
- Time needed ....2 hrs

What I Need:
- Contract clearly stating cancellation and rejection fees
- Client's concept sketches
- Time needed ....1 hr

Total Time
Required..........................3 hrs

YOUR HOURS

What You Know:
-
-
-
- Time needed ...._____hrs

What You Need:
-
-
- Time needed ...._____hrs

Total Time
Required ...._____hrs

4 CLIENT REQUIREMENTS

TURN PAGE

EXAMPLE

What I Know:
- The rendering will be presented at different times to the board of directors, trustees and major donors
- Illustration will be used in a fund-raising brochure
- I must provide a 4 x 5-inch transparency for color separation
- Time needed ....2 hrs

What I Need:
- Written agreement covering billable expenses and limitations on revision rounds
- Time needed ....1 hr

Total Time Required............................**3 hrs**

YOUR HOURS

What You Know:
-
-
-
- Time needed ...._____hrs

What You Need:
-
- Time needed ...._____hrs

Total Time Required............_____hrs

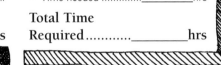

5 DEVELOP SKETCHES

EXAMPLE

What I Know:
- Two different perspective sketches for client review
- Computer drawings of selected view
- Color palette and entourage: people, trees, site furnishings & landscaping to scale
- Time needed ....10 hrs

What I Need:
- Prompt client approval and selection of view to be rendered
- Time for another round of client reviews
- Time needed ....5 hrs

Total Time Required............................**15 hrs**

YOUR HOURS

What You Know:
-
-
-
- Time needed ...._____hrs

What You Need:
-
-
- Time needed ...._____hrs

Total Time Required............_____hrs

7 CLIENT MEETINGS

EXAMPLE

What I Know:
- Review preliminary drawings
- Approval of computer sketch
- Approval of revisions
- Approval of completed rendering
- Time needed ....3 hrs

What I Need:
- Approval/change forms for client signature
- Time needed ....1 hr

Total Time Required ....**4 hrs**

YOUR HOURS

What You Know:
-
-
-
-
- Time needed ...._____hrs

What You Need:
-
- Time needed ...._____hrs

Total Time Required............_____hrs

6 DEVELOP FINISHED ILLUSTRATION

EXAMPLE

What I Know:
- Produce finished watercolor rendering
- Mount on gray board with tissue overlay
- Time needed ....12 hrs

What I Need:
- 4 x 5 color transparency
- Time needed ....1 hr

Total Time Required ....**13 hrs**

YOUR HOURS

What You Know:
-
-
- Time needed ...._____hrs

What You Need:
-
- Time needed ...._____hrs

Total Time Required............_____hrs

WORKSHEET 29 CONTINUED

8 PAPERWORK

EXAMPLE
What I Know:
- Prepare estimate of my fee
- Develop work schedule
- Prepare invoice
- Time needed ....1 hr

What I Need:
- Itemization of billable expenses
- Time needed ....1 hr

Total Time
Required ....2 hrs

YOUR HOURS
What You Know:
-
-
-
- Time needed..............._____hrs

What You Need:
-
- Time needed..............._____hrs

Total Time
Required ...._____hrs

9 TOTAL PROJECT HOURS

EXAMPLE
- Total the hours in Boxes 2-8 to estimate number of project hours ....44 hrs

YOUR HOURS
-

10 HIDDEN SURPRISES

EXAMPLE
- Multiply the amount in Box 9 by .10 (10%) to guard against Hidden Surprises and add that to the amount in Box 9 ....48 hrs
(44 x .10 = 4, then 44 + 4 = 48)
(Build a margin into your estimate to avoid cost overruns that anger clients or cost you money.)

YOUR HOURS
-

12 URGENCY OF JOB

EXAMPLE
What I Know:
- Overtime will be necessary to meet client's tight deadline
- Time needed ....15 hrs
- Rush charge $30/hr

What I Need:
- Nothing additional
- Time needed ....0 hrs/$0
- Rush charge ....0%/$0

Total Time Required/Total
Rush Costs...........10 hrs/$450
- (For a rush project, add your usual percentage for overtime or rush work. Most illustrators charge at least time-and-a-half for working around the clock or over a holiday. Adding an additional percentage for overtime to the total is also common; the Total Project Hours would be multiplied by a percentage for the rush charge: 10 hours x $60/hr = $600 + (600 x .05 (5%)) = $630.00 total.)

YOUR COSTS
What You Know:
-
- Time needed ...._____hrs
- Rush charge ....$_____/hr

What You Need:
-
- Time needed ...._____hrs/$_____
- Rush charge......._____%/$_____

Total Time Required/Total
Rush Costs ..._____hrs/$_____
-

11 TIME & WORK FEE

EXAMPLE
- Multiply the total hours by your hourly rate (48 hrs x $60) $2,880

YOUR COSTS
-

13 EXPENSES

EXAMPLE
What I Know:
- Travel $175
- Transparency 25
- Site photographs....................50
- Subtotal $250
- Markup (15%) 37.50
  (Architectural illustrators typically charge a markup; whether you do or don't, be consistent in your practice.)

Total **$287.50**

What I Need:
- Margin for Extra Costs (10%) $28.70
  (287 x .10 = $28.70)
- Get written agreement specifying that expenses are billed separately. (Always try to negotiate that expenses be billed separately from your fee, in case unexpected expenses arise. Whenever additional expenses are incurred, notify the client immediately. If a client doesn't sign off on the expense at the time it's incurred, he may refuse to pay it on your invoice.)

Total Expenses.....................$316

YOUR COSTS
What You Know:
-
-
-
-
-

Total ....$_____

What You Need:
-
-

Total Expenses ...$_____

15 TOTAL PROJECT COSTS

EXAMPLE
- Total Boxes 11, 12, 13 and 14 and then round up to the nearest fifth or tenth dollar $3,646
- Sales Tax
  (Calculate sales tax only for the final invoice since it has to be figured on actual costs.)

YOUR COSTS
-
-

GOAL

14 RIGHTS SOLD

EXAMPLE
What I Know:
- First reproduction rights only
- If artwork is to be used for other than its original purposes, the usage price will be negotiated
- Original artwork will be returned

Usage Fee $0

YOUR COSTS
What You Know:
-
-
-

Usage Fee ....$_____

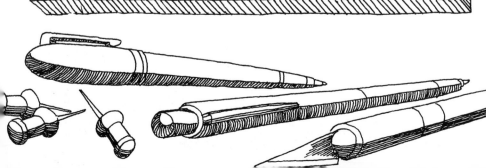

WORKSHEET 30

NEWSPAPER CARTOONS

In this worksheet, a syndicate offers a cartoonist a development contract (with a flat fee) to produce what's called a "workable property" based on the artist's ideas. If the work is considered salable, the cartoonist receives a contract and the syndicate distributes the property. The standard split of the distribution profits is at least 50/50.

To arrive at an estimate for an assignment, fill in the amounts requested as you move through the gameboard. Skip boxes that do not apply, but otherwise go in order until you reach the goal. An example has been given for you to follow in coming up with your own figures.

START

1 TYPE OF PROJECT—SYNDICATED SINGLE-PANEL

Client Name: Cartoon Service
Type & Size of Client: Syndicate serving 1,600 daily, weekly and
 monthly newspapers
Subject Matter: Parenting
Style: B&W line drawings
Medium: Pen & ink
Time: 3 months
Budget: $2,000-4,000

3 INITIAL CLIENT MEETING

EXAMPLE

What I Know:
- Phone meeting to discuss/revise my ideas/samples/style
- Discussion of current parenting trends/issues
- Time needed ....1 hr

What I Need:
- Faxed samples of the syndicate editor's character ideas
- Samples of other cartoons on the topic of parenting
- Time needed ....1 hr

Total Time
Required ....2 hrs

YOUR HOURS

What You Know:
-
-
- Time needed ...._____hrs

What You Need:
-
-
- Time needed...................._____hrs

Total Time
Required ...._____hrs

2 COMPLEXITY OF JOB

EXAMPLE

What I Know:
- Development contract requires 3-6 weeks' worth of cartoons
- Time needed ....5 hrs

What I Need:
- To get parenting material (from magazines, newspapers, etc.)
- Development contract
- Time needed ....3 hrs

Total Time
Required ....8 hrs

YOUR HOURS

What You Know:
-
- Time needed ...._____hrs

What You Need:
-
- Time needed...................._____hrs

Total Time
Required ...._____hrs

4 CLIENT REQUIREMENTS

EXAMPLE

What I Know:
- Syndicate has good reputation
- This is only a development agreement
- Write gags and develop sketches in pencil for initial review
- Time needed ....3 hrs

What I Need:
- Determine syndicate's financial and usage terms
- Research success of syndicate's other cartoons
- Time needed ....1 hr

Total Time
Required ....4 hrs

YOUR HOURS

What You Know:
-
-
-
- Time needed ...._____hrs

What You Need:
-
-
- Time needed ...._____hrs

Total Time
Required............_____hrs

TURN PAGE

7 CLIENT MEETINGS

EXAMPLE

What I Know:
- Phone meeting to discuss initial sketch ideas
- Phone meeting to discuss revisions
- Phone meeting to discuss artwork
- Client needs to sign approval/change form for all stages
- Time needed ....3 hrs

What I Need:
- Consult with a copyright lawyer to discuss terms
- Time needed ....1 hr

Total Time
Required ....4 hrs

YOUR HOURS

What You Know:
-
-
-
- Time needed ...._____hrs

What You Need:
-
- Time needed ...._____hrs

Total Time
Required............_____hrs

5 DEVELOP SKETCHES

EXAMPLE

What I Know:
- Client wants 2-3 ideas/gags and all characters in pencil form
- Client wants to see/approve original drawings of characters
- Send all artwork by mail
- Time needed ....5 hrs

What I Need:
- Retain copies of the originals
- Approval/change forms in hand before finalizing the panels
- Time needed ....1 hr

Total Time
Required ....6 hrs

YOUR HOURS

What You Know:
-
-
-
- Time needed ...._____hrs

What You Need:
-
-
- Time needed ...._____hrs

Total Time
Required............_____hrs

6 DEVELOP FINISHED ILLUSTRATION

EXAMPLE

What I Know:
- Begin final panels based on client selection/revisions
- Client gets originals; I keep copies
- Time needed................................20 hrs

What I Need:
- Allow for additional editorial revisions
- Time needed................................4 hrs

Total Time
Required ....24 hrs

YOUR HOURS

What You Know:
-
-
- Time needed ...._____hrs

What You Need:
-
- Time needed ...._____hrs

Total Time
Required............_____hrs

WORKSHEET 30 CONTINUED

8 PAPERWORK

EXAMPLE

What I Know:
- Prepare estimate and document time and costs for tax records
- Put together work schedule
- Time needed ....1 hr

What I need:
- Review development contract with attorney
- Time needed ....1 hr

Total Time Required...........................2 hrs

YOUR HOURS

What You Know:
-
-
- Time needed..............._____hrs

What You Need:
-
- Time needed ...._____hrs

Total Time Required ...._____hrs

9 TOTAL PROJECT HOURS

EXAMPLE
- Total the hours in Boxes 2-8 to estimate project hours ....50 hrs

YOUR HOURS
-

10 HIDDEN SURPRISES

EXAMPLE
- Multiply the amount in Box 9 by .10 (10%) to guard against Hidden Surprises; add that to the amount in Box 9 ....55 hrs
(50 x .10 = 5, then 50 + 5 = 55)
(Build a margin into your estimate to avoid cost overruns that anger clients or cost you money.)

YOUR HOURS
-

12 URGENCY OF JOB

EXAMPLE

What I Know:
- Schedule is manageable; no overtime
- Time needed ....0 hrs
- Rush charge ....0%/$0

What I Need:
- Nothing else is needed
- Time needed ....0 hrs/$0
- Rush charge ....0%/$0

Total Time Required/Total Rush Costs................0 hrs/$0
- (For a rush project, add your usual percentage for overtime or rush work. Most illustrators charge at least time-and-a-half for working around the clock or over a holiday. Adding an additional percentage for overtime to the total is also common; the Total Project Hours would be multiplied by a percentage for the rush charge: 10 hours x $60/hr = $600 + (600 x .05 (5%)) = $630.00 total.)

YOUR COSTS

What You Know:
-
- Time needed ...._____hrs
- Rush charge......._____%/$_____

What You Need:
-
- Time needed ...._____hrs/$_____
- Rush charge........._____%/$_____

Total Time Required/Total Rush Costs ....._____hrs/$____
-

11 TIME & WORK FEE

EXAMPLE
- Multiply the total hours by your hourly rate (55 hours x $60) $3,330

YOUR COSTS
-

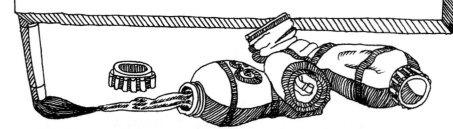

13 EXPENSES

EXAMPLE

What I Know:
- Materials.............................$25
- Photocopies............................5
- Mailing 10
- Subtotal $40
- Markup (0%) 0
  (Expenses are not billed separately since this is a flat fee situation. Not all artists charge markup; whether you do or don't, be consistent in your practice.)

Total $40

What I Need:
- Itemization of my expenses for tax purposes
  (Always try to negotiate billing expenses separately from a flat fee in case unexpected expenses arise. Whenever additional expenses are incurred, notify the client immediately. If a client doesn't sign off on the expense at the time it's incurred, he may refuse to pay it on your invoice.)

Total Expenses.....................$40

YOUR COSTS

What You Know:
-
-
-
-
-

Total ....$_____

What You Need:
-

Total Expenses ...$_____

15 TOTAL PROJECT COSTS

GOAL

EXAMPLE
- Total Boxes 11, 12, 13 and 14 and then round up to the nearest fifth or tenth dollar $3,340
- Sales Tax
  (Calculate sales tax only for the final invoice since it has to be figured on actual costs.)

YOUR COSTS
-

-

14 RIGHTS SOLD

EXAMPLE

What I Know:
- Rights sold will be determined at time of distribution
- If a syndication contract is offered, copyright, reproduction rights and sales split will be negotiated at that time

Usage Fee $0
- (Since this is a development contract, you'll get royalties as your usage fee; that's not calculated here. If your work isn't accepted, it won't be used. So there won't be a usage fee.)

YOUR COSTS

What You Know:
-

-

Usage Fee ....$_____
-

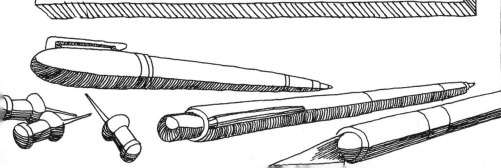

WORKSHEET 31

GREETING CARD ILLUSTRATIONS

Greeting card illustrations pay either a flat fee or a royalty (with a possible advance on royalties). This worksheet shows how to estimate a project that pays an advance and a royalty (a percentage of wholesale or retail price). Before accepting any arrangement, determine whether the projected earnings will pay a substantial profit over and above your cost in time and materials.

To determine if you are being fairly paid, fill in the amounts requested as you move through the gameboard. Skip boxes that do not apply, but otherwise go in order until you reach the goal. An example has been given for you to follow in coming up with your own figures.

START

1 TYPE OF PROJECT—GREETING CARD ILLUSTRATIONS

Client Name: Heartfelt Creations
Type & Size of Client: Medium-sized greeting card company
Subject Matter: Friend's birthday
Style: Loose, whimsical
Medium: Watercolor
Budget: $500 advance + 4% royalty
Time: 1 month

3 INITIAL CLIENT MEETING

EXAMPLE

What I Know:
- Meet with owner and art director
- Discuss slant, look, market and card specs
- Time needed....................................1 hr

What I Need:
- Contract clearly stating advance, royalty and payment schedule
- Advance paid half on signing, half on delivery of artwork
- Time needed....................................1 hr

Total Time Required ....2 hrs

YOUR HOURS

What You Know:
-
-
- Time needed ...._____hrs

What You Need:
-
-
- Time needed ...._____hrs

Total Time Required ...._____hrs

2 COMPLEXITY OF JOB

EXAMPLE

What I Know:
- Create 4 illustrations on theme
- Client supplies editorial
- Must not require elaborate production
- Client wants to choose from 2 color sketches for each card
- Time needed...................................1 hr

What I Need:
- Samples of other cards in this line and competitive card lines
- Client's conceptual guidelines
- Time needed ....2 hrs

Total Time Required..........................3 hrs

YOUR HOURS

What You Know:
-
-
-
-
- Time needed ...._____hrs

What You Need:
-
-
- Time needed ...._____hrs

Total Time Required ...._____hrs

4 CLIENT REQUIREMENTS

PRICING DESIGN & ILLUSTRATION PROJECTS **131**

TURN PAGE

EXAMPLE

What I Know:
- Production requirement must be simple
- Blank area must be left for editorial on cover
- Client wants transparencies for reproduction
- Time needed ....1½ hrs

What I Need:
- Client's creative guidelines for artwork
- Time needed...................................½ hr

Total Time Required..............................**2 hrs**

YOUR HOURS

What You Know:
-
-
-
- Time needed ...._____hrs

What You Need:
-
- Time needed ...._____hrs

Total Time Required............._____**hrs**

7 CLIENT MEETINGS

EXAMPLE

What I Know:
- Meeting to discuss/review sketches and color ideas
- Meeting to discuss/revise/approve finished art
- Send approval/change form with final art
- Deliver final art
- Time needed ....2 hrs

What I Need:
- Approval/change forms for client
- Time needed ....1 hr

Total Time Required ....**3 hrs**

YOUR HOURS

What You Know:
-
-
-
-
- Time needed ...._____hrs

What You Need:
-
- Time needed ...._____hrs

Total Time Required............._____**hrs**

5 DEVELOP SKETCHES

EXAMPLE

What I Know:
- Client wants 2 rough sketches for each card
- Client wants to see colors notations
- Time needed ....8 hrs

What I Need:
- Fax rough sketches to client for review
- Discuss revisions
- Time needed ....1 hr

Total Time Required..............................**9 hrs**

YOUR HOURS

What You Know:
-
-
- Time needed ...._____hrs

What You Need:
-
-
- Time needed ...._____hrs

Total Time Required............._____**hrs**

6 DEVELOP FINISHED ILLUSTRATION

EXAMPLE

What I Know:
- Sketches approved
- Develop finished illustrations for each
- Send approval/change form with final artwork
- Time needed ....8 hrs

What I Need:
- Deliver original art for transparency
- Keep color copies of finished pieces
- Time needed ....2 hrs

Total Time Required ....**10 hrs**

YOUR HOURS

What You Know:
-
-
-
- Time needed ...._____hrs

What You Need:
-
-
- Time needed ...._____hrs

Total Time Required............._____**hrs**

WORKSHEET 31 CONTINUED

8 PAPERWORK

EXAMPLE

What I Know:
- Review contract
- Estimate costs to see if advance will cover time and expenses
- Prepare work schedule
- Time needed ....1 hr

What I Need:
- Lawyer to review contract
- Check for the advance
- Time needed ....1 hr

Total Time Required ....2 hrs

YOUR HOURS

What You Know:
-
-
-
- Time needed..............._____hrs

What You Need:
-
-
- Time needed..............._____hrs

Total Time Required ...._____hrs

9 TOTAL PROJECT HOURS

EXAMPLE
- Total the hours in Boxes 2-8 to estimate project hours ....31 hrs

YOUR HOURS
-

10 HIDDEN SURPRISES

EXAMPLE
- Multiply the amount in Box 9 by .10 (10%) to guard against Hidden Surprises and add that to the amount in Box 9 ....34 hrs
  (31 x .10 = 3, then 31 + 3 = 34)
  (Build a margin into your estimate to avoid cost overruns that anger clients or cost you money.)

YOUR HOURS
-

12 URGENCY OF JOB

EXAMPLE

What I Know:
- Deadline is manageable, no overtime needed
- Time needed ....0 hrs
- Rush charge ....0%/$0

What I Need:
- Agreement that finished artwork is due 10 days after client approval
- Time needed ....0 hrs/$0
- Rush charge ....0%/$0

Total Time Required/Total Rush Costs ....0 hrs/$0
- (For a rush project, add your usual percentage for overtime or rush work. Most illustrators charge at least time-and-a-half for working around the clock or over a holiday. Adding an additional percentage for overtime to the total is also common; the Total Project Hours would be multiplied by a percentage for the rush charge: 10 hours x $60/hr = $600 + (600 x .05 (5%)) = $630.00 total.)

YOUR COSTS

What You Know:
-
- Time needed.................._____hrs
- Rush charge......._____%/$_____

What You Need:
-
- Time needed......._____hrs/$_____
- Rush charge........._____%/$_____

Total Time Required/Total Rush Costs ..._____hrs/$_____
-

11 TIME & WORK FEE

EXAMPLE
- Multiply the total hours by your hourly rate (34 hrs x $60) $2,040

YOUR COSTS
-

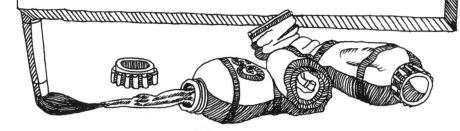

13 EXPENSES

EXAMPLE
What I Know:
- C-print/color photocopies..................$25
- Supplies...............................10
- Drawing papers 15
- Faxes 12
- Subtotal $62
- Markup (0%) 0
  (No markup is charged since payment is a royalty advance, which must cover expenses. Not all artists charge markup; whether you do or don't, be consistent in your practice.)

Total $62

What I Need:
- Margin for Extra Costs (10%) $6
  (When initial payment for a job is a small royalty advance, try to negotiate for the client to pay expenses. As soon as new expenses are incurred during a project, notify the client. If a client doesn't sign off on the expense at the time it's incurred, he may refuse to pay it later. If a client won't pay expenses out of pocket, he may be willing to reimburse you for them out of your future royalties.)

Total Expenses.....................$68

YOUR COSTS
What You Know:
-
-
-
-
-
-

Total ....$_____

What You Need:
-

Total Expenses ...$_____

15 TOTAL PROJECT COSTS

EXAMPLE
- Total Boxes 11, 12, 13 and 14 and then round up to the nearest fifth or tenth dollar $2,108
  (You only recoup $1/4$ of your time and costs from the advance, so the decision to go ahead will depend on your estimate of the greeting card company's ability to market the cards.)

YOUR COSTS
-

GOAL

14 RIGHTS SOLD

EXAMPLE
What I Know:
- Client wants exclusive greeting card, stationery and giftwrap rights
- Original artwork to be returned to me
- Term of agreement is 2 years
- Additional usage will be negotiated
- I retain copyright
- Client is offering $500 plus 4% royalties

Usage Fee............$500 plus 4% royalties
- (Since it's not known how much more than $500 you'll earn, the usage fee is not part of the calculation in the next box.)

YOUR COSTS
What You Know:
-
-
-
-
-
-

Usage Fee ....$_____
-

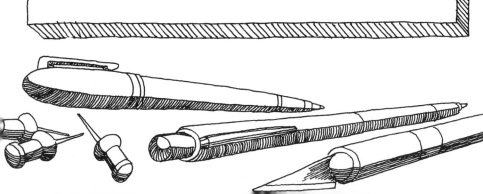

WORKSHEET 32

BUSINESS/INSTITUTIONAL ILLUSTRATION

This example demonstrates pricing illustrations for a corporate in-house booklet. In this case, the illustrator works on an hourly fee basis, since the project is too complex to risk doing for a flat fee. It is crucial to get in writing that you will bill expenses separately and will retain ownership of the art. The contract should also state how the art will be used.

To arrive at an estimate for an assignment, fill in the amounts requested as you move through the gameboard. Skip boxes that do not apply, but otherwise go in order until you reach the goal. An example has been given for you to follow in coming up with your own figures.

START

1 TYPE OF PROJECT—EMPLOYEE BOOKLET ILLUSTRATIONS

Client Name: City Bank
Type & Size of Client: Local midsized city savings institution
Subject Matter: Bank personnel interacting with customers
Style: Detailed, crisply rendered, line and tone
Medium: Ink and wash
Time: 2 weeks
Budget: $7,000-8,000

3 INITIAL CLIENT MEETING

EXAMPLE
What I Know:
- Discuss client's goal for the booklet
- Review examples of art style client wants
- Discuss concepts
- Time needed..............................3 hrs

What I Need:
- To get competitors' motivational booklets
- To observe day-to-day operations at the bank
- Time needed.................................4 hrs

Total Time Required..........................7 hrs

YOUR HOURS
What You Know:
-
-
-
- Time needed..................._____hrs

What You Need:
-
-
- Time needed..................._____hrs

Total Time Required.............._____hrs

2 COMPLEXITY OF JOB

EXAMPLE
What I Know:
- Illustrations for a 32-page booklet
- Consists of 1 b&w cover drawing with a second-color overlay; 3 full-page, b&w drawings; 16 b&w spot drawings
- Client will supply photo references
- Time needed ....5 hrs

What I Need:
- Samples of illustrations used before
- Booklet copy
- Contract clearly stating kill fees
- Time needed ....2 hrs

Total Time Required..........................7 hrs

YOUR HOURS
What You Know:
-
-
- Time needed ...._____hrs

What You Need:
-
-
-
- Time needed ...._____hrs

Total Time Required.............._____hrs

4 CLIENT REQUIREMENTS

EXAMPLE

What I Know:
- Client wants rough sketches prior to final art
- Finished illustrations need to be very polished
- Time needed ....20 hrs

What I Need:
- Client's reference photos
- Booklet's page layouts showing size and placement of art
- Time needed ....1 hr

**Total Time
Required**...........................**21 hrs**

YOUR HOURS

What You Know:
-
-
- Time needed ...._____hrs

What You Need:
-
-
- Time needed ...._____hrs

**Total Time
Required**............_____**hrs**

5 DEVELOP SKETCHES

EXAMPLE

What I Know:
- 2 thumbnail roughs for each illustration
- 1 rough sketch to size for each illustration
- Client will review faxed sketches prior to initial meeting
- Time needed ....24 hrs

What I Need:
- Agreed to schedule for client changes and my revisions
- Study photos before beginning
- Time needed ....1 hr

**Total Time
Required**...........................**25 hrs**

YOUR HOURS

What You Know:
-
-
-
- Time needed ...._____hrs

What You Need:
-
-
- Time needed ...._____hrs

**Total Time
Required**............_____**hrs**

TURN PAGE

7 CLIENT MEETINGS

EXAMPLE

What I Know:
- Review/approval of rough sketches
- Review/approval of completed illustrations
- Delivery of finished art
- Send approval/change form with all stages of art
- Time needed ....3 hrs

What I Need:
- Contracts and approval/change forms for client signature
- Time needed ....1 hr

**Total Time
Required** ....**4 hrs**

YOUR HOURS

What You Know:
-
-
-
-
- Time needed ...._____hrs

What You Need:
-
- Time needed ...._____hrs

**Total Time
Required**............_____**hrs**

6 DEVELOP FINISHED ILLUSTRATION

EXAMPLE

What I Know:
- Sketches approved; complete final illustrations
- Will need final approval before sending finished art
- Time needed...............................35 hrs

What I Need:
- Stats & photocopies of each illustration; second-color overlay
- Time needed..................................3 hrs

**Total Time
Required** ....**38 hrs**

YOUR HOURS

What You Know:
-
-
- Time needed ...._____hrs

What You Need:
-
- Time needed ...._____hrs

**Total Time
Required**............_____**hrs**

WORKSHEET 32 *CONTINUED*

8 PAPERWORK

EXAMPLE

What I Know:
- Develop work schedule
- Prepare invoice
- Document expenses
- Time needed ....3 hrs

What I Need:
- Get in writing that expenses will be billed separately
- Agree to hourly rate
- Time needed ....1 hr

Total Time Required............................**4 hrs**

YOUR HOURS

What You Know:
-
-
-
- Time needed................_____hrs

What You Need:
-
-
- Time needed................_____hrs

Total Time Required ...._____**hrs**

9 TOTAL PROJECT HOURS

EXAMPLE
- Total the hours in Boxes 2-8 to estimate project hours ....106 hrs

YOUR HOURS
-

10 HIDDEN SURPRISES

EXAMPLE
- Multiply the amount in Box 9 by .10 (10%) to guard against Hidden Surprises; add that to the amount in Box 9 ....117 hrs
  (106 x .10 = 11, then 106 + 11 = 117)
  (Build a margin into your estimate to avoid cost overruns that anger clients or cost you money.)

YOUR HOURS
-

12 URGENCY OF JOB

EXAMPLE

What I Know:
- Time is adequate if only 2 rounds of revisions
- Time needed ....0 hrs
- Rush charge ....0%/$0

What I Need:
- Is deadline firm?
- Are more than 2 rounds of revisions expected?
- Time needed.........................0 hrs/$0
- Rush charge.........................0 hrs/$0

Total Time Required/Total Rush Costs..................**0 hrs/$0**
- (For a rush project, add your usual percentage for overtime or rush work. Most illustrators charge at least time-and-a-half for working around the clock or over a holiday. Adding an additional percentage for overtime to the total is also common; the Total Project Hours would be multiplied by a percentage for the rush charge: 10 hours x $60/hr = $600 + (600 x .05 (5%)) = $630.00 total.)

YOUR COSTS

What You Know:
-
- Time needed ...._____hrs
- Rush charge......._____%/$_____

What You Need:
-
-
- Time needed ...._____hrs/$_____
- Rush charge........_____hrs/$_____

Total Time Required/Total Rush Costs ..._____hrs/$_____
-

11 TIME & WORK FEE

EXAMPLE
- Multiply the total hours by your hourly rate (117 hrs x $60).................$7,020

YOUR COSTS
-

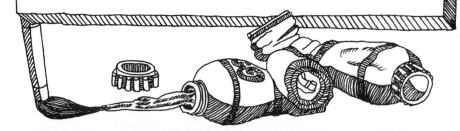

13 EXPENSES

EXAMPLE

What I Know:
- Stats/photocopies $85
- Supplies..50
- Subtotal $135
- Markup (20%). 27
  (Some artists charge 20-25% markup on expenses under $1,000 and 15% on expenses over $1,000. Whether you do or don't charge a markup, be consistent in your practice.)

Total $162

What I Need:
- Margin for Extra Costs (10%) $16
  (162 x .10 = $16.20)
- Get written agreement that expenses are separate from fee.
  (Always try to negotiate that expenses be billed separately from your fee, in case unexpected expenses arise. If additional expenses are incurred, notify the client immediately. If a client doesn't sign off on the expense at the time it's incurred, he may refuse to pay it on your invoice.)

Total Expenses....................$178

YOUR COSTS

What You Know:
-
-
-
-

Total ....$_____

What You Need:
-
-

Total Expenses ...$_____

15 TOTAL PROJECT COSTS

EXAMPLE
- Total Boxes 11, 12, 13 and 14 and then round up to the nearest fifth or tenth dollar $7,198
- Sales Tax
  (Calculate sales tax only for the final invoice since it has to be figured on actual costs.)

YOUR COSTS
-
-

GOAL

14 RIGHTS SOLD

EXAMPLE

What I Know:
- One time reproduction rights are for the booklet only
- If artwork is to be used for other purposes, the price will be renegotiated
- Original artwork will be retained by me

Usage Fee $0

YOUR COSTS

What You Know:
-
-
-

Usage Fee ....$_____

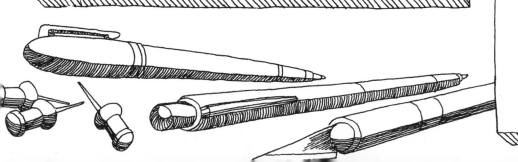

WORKSHEET 33

COMPUTER GRAPHICS

This example involves pricing computer-generated illustrations. The factors to consider in a project like this are the number of hours the illustrations will take to execute, the usage rights, whether you charge a computer usage fee in addition to your hourly creative fee, and whether you are responsible for output. If buying new software is necessary, that too must be included in the billable expenses.

To arrive at an estimate for an assignment, fill in the amounts requested as you move through the gameboard. Skip boxes that do not apply, but otherwise go in order until you reach the goal. An example has been given for you to follow in coming up with your own figures.

START

1 TYPE OF PROJECT—COMPUTER GRAPHICS

Client Name: Bradford Industries
Type & Size of Client: Large tool & die company specializing in decorative stamped ornaments
Subject Matter: Product renderings
Style: Precise line drawings with some patterned texture
Medium: Computer
Time: 3 weeks
Budget: $4,000-5,000

3 INITIAL CLIENT MEETING

EXAMPLE	YOUR HOURS
What I Know:	**What You Know:**
• Review the ornaments; discuss desired illustration style	•
• Discuss how to render ornaments' textures	•
• Review sales packet layout	•
• Time needed....................................1 hr	• Time needed ...._____hrs
What I Need:	**What You Need:**
• Samples of previous packets	•
• Contract clearly stating kill fees	•
• Time needed...................................1 hr	• Time needed ...._____hrs
Total Time	**Total Time**
Required ....2 hrs	Required ...._____hrs

2 COMPLEXITY OF JOB

EXAMPLE	YOUR HOURS
What I Know:	**What You Know:**
• Illustrations of ornament designs will be used in a sales presentation packet	•
• 5 b&w quarter-page illustrations; 6 b&w spot illustrations	•
• 5 ornaments drawn to scale to display their 3-D quality	•
• Time needed ....3 hrs	• Time needed ...._____hrs
What I Need:	**What You Need:**
• The stamped ornaments	•
• Sell copy accompanying the art	•
• Time needed...............................½ hr	• Time needed ...._____hrs
Total Time	**Total Time**
Required......................3½ hrs	Required................_____hrs

4 CLIENT REQUIREMENTS

TURN PAGE

EXAMPLE

What I Know:
- Client wants printed copies of each drawing
- Client does not want the disk
- Project will not involve text or any other design considerations
- Time needed ....2 hrs

What I Need:
- Revision time after first sketches are reviewed and approved
- Dimensions for art
- Time needed ....5 hrs

Total Time Required..............................7 hrs

YOUR HOURS

What You Know:
-
-
-
- Time needed ...._____hrs

What You Need:
-
-
- Time needed ...._____hrs

Total Time Required..........._____hrs

7 CLIENT MEETINGS

EXAMPLE

What I Know:
- Approval/revision meeting for initial drawings
- Approval/revision meeting for final drawings
- Delivery of finished work and approval/change forms
- Time needed ....3 hrs

What I Need:
- Approval/change forms for client signature
- Time needed ....1 hr

Total Time Required ....4 hrs

YOUR HOURS

What You Know:
-
-
-
- Time needed ...._____hrs

What You Need:
-
- Time needed ...._____hrs

Total Time Required..........._____hrs

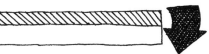

5 DEVELOP SKETCHES

EXAMPLE

What I Know:
- Develop 11 rough drawings
- Must print out drawings and fax to client for review
- Time needed ....10 hrs

What I Need:
- Prompt response from client; approval of textures
- Revision time
- Time needed ....4 hrs

Total Time Required..........................14 hrs

YOUR HOURS

What You Know:
-
-
- Time needed ...._____hrs

What You Need:
-
-
- Time needed ...._____hrs

Total Time Required..........._____hrs

6 DEVELOP FINISHED ILLUSTRATION

EXAMPLE

What I Know:
- Complete final illustrations based on sketch revisions
- Mount art on gray board with tissue overlay
- Time needed ....12 hrs

What I Need:
- Good quality output for client review
- Time needed ....3 hrs

Total Time Required ....15 hrs

YOUR HOURS

What You Know:
-
-
- Time needed ...._____hrs

What You Need:
-
- Time needed ...._____hrs

Total Time Required..........._____hrs

WORKSHEET 33 *CONTINUED*

8 PAPERWORK

EXAMPLE
What I Know:
- Prepare estimate of my fee
- Prepare estimate of & document expenses
- Prepare work schedule
- Prepare invoice
- Time needed ....2 hrs

What I Need:
- Get in writing that expenses will be billed separately
- Client's budget
- Time needed ....1 hr

Total Time Required ....3 hrs

YOUR HOURS
What You Know:
-
-
-
-
- Time needed............._____hrs

What You Need:
-
-
- Time needed..............._____hrs

Total Time Required ...._____hrs

9 TOTAL PROJECT HOURS

EXAMPLE
- Total the hours in Boxes 2-8 to estimate project hours ....48.5 hrs

YOUR HOURS
-

10 HIDDEN SURPRISES

EXAMPLE
- Multiply the amount in Box 9 by .10 (10%) to guard against Hidden Surprises; add that to the amount in Box 9 ....53.5 hrs
  (48.5 x .10 = 5, then 48.5 + 5 = 53.5)
  (Build a margin into your estimate to avoid cost overruns that anger clients or cost you money.)

YOUR HOURS
-

12 URGENCY OF JOB

EXAMPLE
What I Know:
- Deadline is manageable
- Time needed ....0 hrs
- Rush charge ....0%/$0

What I Need:
- A written agreement limiting the number of revisions
- Whether deadline is firm
- Time needed ....0 hrs/$0
- Rush charge ....0%/$0

Total Time Required/Total Rush Costs.................0 hrs/$0
- (For a rush project, add your usual percentage for overtime or rush work. Most illustrators charge at least time-and-a-half for working around the clock or over a holiday. Adding an additional percentage for overtime to the total is also common; the Total Project Hours would be multiplied by a percentage for the rush charge: 18 hours x $50/hr = $900 + (900 x .05 (5%)) = $945.00 total.)

YOUR COSTS
What You Know:
-
- Time needed ...._____hrs
- Rush charge........_____%/$_____

What You Need:
-
-
- Time needed......._____hrs/$_____
- Rush charge........._____%/$_____

Total Time Required/Total Rush Costs ..._____hrs/$_____
-

11 TIME & WORK FEE

EXAMPLE
- Multiply the total hours by your hourly rate (53.5 x $60) $3,210

YOUR COSTS
-

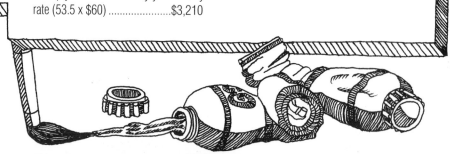

13 EXPENSES

EXAMPLE
What I Know:
- Computer Usage $350
- Linotronic conversion 150
- Computer software............................195
- Subtotal $695
- Markup (15%) 104.25
  (Many artists charge a markup of 20-25% on expenses under $1,000 and 15% on expenses over $1,000. Whether you charge a markup or not, be consistent in your practice.)

Total $799.25

What I Need:
- Margin for Extra Costs (5%) $40
  (799.25 x .05 = $40) ($39.96 rounded up)
- Get written agreement that expenses are billed separately.
  (Always try to negotiate that expenses be billed separately from your fee, in case unexpected expenses arise. If additional expenses are incurred, notify the client immediately. If a client doesn't sign off on the expense at the time it's incurred, he may refuse to pay it on your invoice.)

Total Expenses $839.25

YOUR COSTS
What You Know:
-
-
-
-
-

Total ....$_____

What You Need:
-
-

Total Expenses ...$_____

15 TOTAL PROJECT COSTS

EXAMPLE
- Total Boxes 11, 12, 13 and 14 and then round up to the nearest fifth or tenth dollar $4,050
- Sales Tax
  (Calculate sales tax only for the final invoice since it has to be figured on actual costs.)

YOUR COSTS
-
-

14 RIGHTS SOLD

EXAMPLE
What I Know:
- Fee covers use in sales packet only
- Other future uses must be renegotiated
- Client buys exclusive rights for using this art in the packet

Usage Fee $0

YOUR COSTS
What You Know:
-
-
-

Usage Fee ....$_____

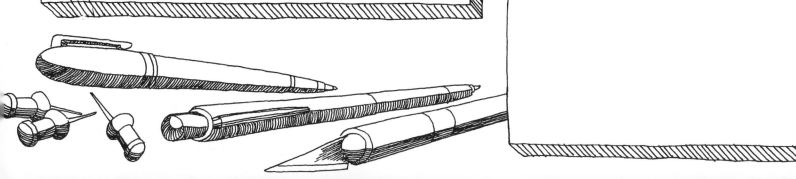

It Takes More Than Good Prices

Being a successful designer or illustrator takes more than good prices. To get more of the work you want, you need a good portfolio, proposal and presentation. You also need to know how to negotiate, stay competitive and get paid.

In this chapter you'll discover how to put together that proposal, presentation and portfolio to get the job you want. I'll review important do's and don'ts for each opportunity to sell your ideas to the client. Once you've gotten a project, you need good negotiation skills to make it go smoothly. We'll look at effective negotiation techniques and ways to handle the two most common client problems—unreasonable deadlines and unrealistic budgets.

Staying competitive doesn't mean being the cheapest talent in town. We'll look at why cutting overhead and increasing your marketing efforts may be smarter than cutting prices. Last, but not least, we'll look at ways to make sure that you get paid when the job is done.

PROPOSALS

A proposal is a detailed explanation of how you will develop and execute a project for a client. Not all projects require a proposal; in fact, many do not. But clients do ask for proposals on larger, more competitive projects like annual reports, signage systems and identity packages. They want to be sure they've chosen the best designer for these complex, long term and high-priced jobs.

Illustrators are seldom asked to prepare proposals, so you illustrators may want to skip over this part. But don't close the book just yet. You'll at least want to look at the information on portfolios (see pages 145-146).

A proposal includes:

1. An opening statement explaining what you know about the project—its goals and objectives.

2. A description of your approach to the project and how that will achieve the client's goals and objectives.

3. A list or outline of the steps you will take to produce the project.

4. A market research report, if required.

5. An itemized budget for the project and a production schedule.

Designers are sometimes asked to work up several creative concepts as fully developed comps to accompany proposals. Many designers refuse to produce a creative product as part of a proposal since they consider that spec work. (This is also the position of the AIGA and the Graphic Artists Guild.) Instead, they show a body of work for similar clients or show projects comparable to the one covered in the proposal.

You have to decide whether to go along with a client's demands and expectations. But make that choice from an informed position. Before you agree to doing conceptual work as part of a proposal, figure out how much time it will take to produce it and whether you can afford to lose that time from paying projects. It's a different story altogether if you've signed a work agreement and the proposal is merely a part of the ongoing project.

How to Prepare a Proposal

You must do your homework to prepare a good proposal. Even when you don't feel you should put a lot of time into one, it must show that you have an understanding of the prospective client's product or service and its customers.

In the opening statement recap what you know about the project. Reiterate its goals and objectives and remind the client of any discussions you've had (an opportunity to show how well you listen).

Describe in general terms the approach you will take to the project. Draw on your research to show your understanding of the client and the market and explain why your approach will produce the results the client wants.

If you must include a market research report in a proposal, produce it as you usually do or bring in a market research consultant to prepare that part.

Outline the work you will do and the timetable for its completion. Rather than itemize each step in the process, many designers break a project into stages. For example, a project might be broken out as "Phase One: Collect information on the new products; Phase Two: Present for approval three design concepts"; etc.

Carefully spell out how many concepts and how many comps the client will see. This shouldn't be more than three or four concepts and even fewer comps. Indicate that there will be extra charges for showing additional concepts or comps or for additional rounds of approval. (And don't forget to mention that client revisions to the piece will be billed in addition to the costs presented in the cost estimate.)

Once you've gotten the specs from the client and decided what form the project will take, you'll need to detail the time and money costs for the clients in your cost estimate. To prepare a cost estimate follow these steps:

1. Find the worksheet in section three of this book that is most like the project you are estimating.

2. If outside services are involved, prepare a written sheet of project specifications and give one to each vendor or subcontractor you want a quote from. Three quotes for each type of service gives you a basis of comparison.

3. When you have selected the service people you will use, include their prices on the blank worksheet.

4. Use the worksheet to figure out how many hours you'll need to spend in each area of the project and enter the amount in the space provided or on a blank copy.

5. When you've completed the worksheet, you will have your cost estimate.

Design your proposal. Use a typeface that is attractive, yet easy to read. Experiment with graphic treatments, but don't overdo it. Use discretion and make all graphic choices appropriate to the material. For an attractive, personalized look, insert each copy of the proposal into a cover or binder with typed labels indicating the company's name, the client's name, the project title and, of course, your name or your business's name and phone number. Some folders also have a place to insert business cards.

Proposal Do's and Don'ts

1. Do get your proposal in on time. That will be the client's first indica-tion of your reliability.

2. Do be specific and to the point.

3. Do use descriptive, but not flowery, words.

4. Do show your understanding of both the project and the client's business and needs.

5. Do make an appointment to hand deliver the proposal to the client.

6. Do keep a master copy.

7. Don't pad it with any unneces-sary words and information.

8. Don't let your proposal go to a client with any typos, misspellings, or grammar or punctuation errors.

9. Don't just staple your proposal together and hand it to a client. Design proposals carefully and package them attractively.

10. Don't ever show a proposal to a colleague or another client, or divulge any information contained within it to anyone. That is a viola-tion of client confidentiality.

PRESENTATIONS

Presentations usually go hand in hand with proposals. You meet with the client and often other staff members to deliver the proposal and verbally present the informa-tion and ideas it contains.

A presentation is one of the most important business activities design-ers and illustrators engage in, and it

should be taken seriously. Give a presentation the same preparation, thought and creativity that a current client would receive.

Proposal presentations can be either formal or informal. The for-mal presentation is made not only to the client but also to other deci-sion-making members of the com-pany. You will often be asked to make this type of presentation when you are competing with other designers for a project. The presen-tation committee, as it is often called, may consist of business part-ners, corporate officers, members of the board of directors, and key peo-ple in the sales, marketing and advertising departments. You will deliver your written proposal and discuss it with the committee. They may ask to see some conceptual work at this time; decide how you will handle the request. You can show work for similar clients or do a capabilities presentation instead.

An informal presentation is a meeting with the client and maybe one or two staffers to talk about the project, review your cost estimate and work schedule. This usually occurs when you have already been offered the project.

Keys to a Great Presentation

1. Use the presentation to reiter-ate and reinforce how the approach

you've taken will accomplish the client's goals and objectives for this project.

2. Make certain you can substan-tiate all factual information in both the presentation and the proposal.

3. Learn as much as you can about the client before the presenta-tion. Anticipate questions that you might be asked and have your answers ready.

4. Be well-prepared and rehearsed, so there are no awkward pauses. Act out your first step into the client's office, what you will say, the questions you will ask. Go through each phase of the presenta-tion, right up to the time you shake hands and leave.

5. If your partner, staff members or a consultant will make the pre-sentation with you, rehearse who will cover what parts of the presen-tation and in what order, and how to signal each other to speed up, slow down, answer a question, etc.

6. Dress in a professional manner that fits your client's style. Wear nice clothes—no jeans and T-shirts—but you don't have to show up in a three-piece suit or a design-er original. If it's a corporate client, dress corporate. If it's a small busi-ness, a jacket and tie or jacket and skirt will do.

7. Ask the client how many peo-ple will be attending the presenta-

tion. Then prepare a proposal packet—a copy of the proposal and marketing report, if applicable, and any related artwork—for each person and insert the material into a folder. You can personalize the proposals by typing each person's name on the folder if you know their names.

8. Distribute the proposal but don't refer to it during the presentation unless there are certain facts or figures you want to point out. Ask everyone not to look through the proposal packets until after the presentation. They can get so wrapped up in reading it that they may never hear a word you say.

9. Begin the presentation by briefly but clearly reviewing the points you make in the proposal in the order they appear. Never read from your proposal. Know the contents well, but don't memorize and recite it word for word.

10. Even though you may have copies of your visual materials in the proposal packet, always present a mounted display of the work. (If you are presenting concepts, show polished layouts or storyboards.) Cover your presentation boards with a heavy paper that can be flipped back when you are ready to talk about that phase of the presentation. This adds an element of surprise and keeps people wondering what they will see.

11. Presentations are performances. Stay within a specific time limit and be fast moving, informative and even enjoyable.

12. Be enthusiastic, positive and up-beat about getting the job, but don't go too far by begging or being aggressive.

13. Be polite and friendly, even if you sense during the presentation that the client isn't warming up to your ideas.

14. If the presentation is at your studio, then light refreshments may be appropriate. Never serve alcohol or messy foods. You should abstain from eating so you don't have to worry about crumbs on your face or greasy fingerprints.

15. Never, never, never smoke during a presentation—even if your clients do.

16. Even if you know or sense that this client is not interested in you, leave your card and any other printed materials you have. Today's "Sorry, we decided to go with someone else" may turn into tomorrow's "A job just came up, and we thought of you."

SHOWING YOUR PORTFOLIO

It's important to have a portfolio with good work that's appropriate for the client you're meeting. But how you present yourself and the portfolio to the client is as important as what's in it. These qualities often carry as much weight as a portfolio full of dazzling work:

Appearance: The way you dress makes a statement about who you are and what's important to you. What most clients look for, consciously or not, is an overall sense of pride in the clothes you wear.

Attitude: How you move and act can say a great deal about you to a casual observer. You may seem nervous, unsure of yourself and unprepared, or you can appear calm, well-prepared, and at ease in a new situation. Before you fly into the office of a potential client, make sure your outward demeanor is as put together as your clothing.

Trust: The client needs to feel, intuitively, that you will deliver what you promise.

THE PERFECT PORTFOLIO

A portfolio is a sample of the ten or fifteen best pieces you've produced within the last few years. Choose examples that demonstrate the full range of your graphic skills and creativity. But include only pieces that address the needs of that prospective client.

Each work in your portfolio must be yours, but you can include something you worked on as part of a group project. Explain what part of the work is yours and give credit to the other team members. Clients like to see how people handle the various stages of a project, so you might show a few concept layouts, a comp and the finished piece.

Never include anything that is dirty, tattered, yellowed or torn. Mount each piece neatly on the same neutral-colored but sturdy backing material—a heavy, matte-finished paper works well—with an even border of approximately two to three inches all around. Arrange several small pieces in an interesting, uncrowded way on a single page. Always use the best portfolio case you can afford.

Rehearse how you will present your portfolio to potential clients. Think of something to say that will briefly explain each piece of work you will show. For example, What was a particular piece attempting to accomplish? Why was your illustration chosen? How does that piece relate to the kind of work your prospective client is interested in?

Do's and Don'ts

1. Do research the client's company before you come to show your portfolio.

2. Don't mention what you know about the company if it doesn't relate to the conversation.

3. Do come prepared with a conversational icebreaker that will set a

comfortable tone for the rest of the meeting.

4. Don't wait for the client to start asking the questions or lead the review.

5. Do dress professionally.

6. Don't overdress.

7. Do keep your portfolio review brief and to the point.

8. Don't show every piece you've ever done.

9. Do keep your comments and answers focused on the client's needs.

10. Don't think about what you can get out of a job; keep focused on what you can do to meet your client's needs.

NEGOTIATION

Negotiation means give and take: You give something to the other person in return for something you take. The best kind of negotiation is a win/win situation—both parties feel like winners by getting something they want.

Always aim to create a win/win situation with a client. If you give everything away without getting something back from the client, you will begin to feel resentful. For example, suppose you offer your client a 25 percent discount on the next project in an effort to correct a mistake you made on this one. Then your client says, "What? I

would expect at least 50 percent off after what you did."

If you agree to 50 percent even if you don't believe that the mistake warrants it, you will feel taken advantage of. But if you negotiate with the client by saying, "I do want to set things right with you, but the best I can afford to do is 35 percent," most clients will happily accept a counter offer, feeling good that they got a little more than your original offer. And you will feel like you won them over without having to give up too much.

Here are some keys to successful negotiation:

• Arrange an uninterrupted, mutually convenient time to talk to the client.

• Listen carefully and try to understand what the client really wants or needs before trying to make yourself understood.

• Have some solutions in mind and be prepared to explain how these benefit the client.

• Always offer less than you are willing to give. Going this route leaves you with more room to come up when the client counters your offer.

• Ask for more than you really want so the other person can talk you down. That leaves your client feeling that she has gained something.

When a Client Wants the Impossible

Sometimes a client wants you to do something that is literally, physically impossible, and it's clear that he hasn't got a clue why this is an unreasonable request. One of the most common problems is deadlines that can't be met. Another is clients who want more design and production quality than their budgets cover.

Unrealistic Deadlines: Before you tell your client that the deadline is impossible and walk away, explore the options. Explain why the deadline is impossible. If you state your concerns in a way that addresses ultimate satisfaction with the end result, rather than focusing on why you can't meet the deadline, the client will often reconsider. Always suggest a workable alternative.

Sometimes clients are unfamiliar with production and have no idea how long things take. It can help to educate them by explaining or demonstrating, whenever possible, exactly how a particular job is done. This will help them see firsthand what's involved and what can happen when a job is rushed.

Occasionally, you will hit a brick wall when a client refuses to budge on a deadline. When this happens, try suggesting changes in the project that will make the deadline

manageable, such as going with a two-color brochure instead of full color. To help sell your point, show some samples of effective, attractive two-color brochures. If you need an added incentive to convince them, explain how much money they can save with a two-color print job. Few clients can resist the "savings" pitch.

Unworkable Budgets: Clients who are unfamiliar with creative fees and production prices may allocate a totally unworkable budget and then blame you if you can't work within it. When you are presented with a budget that's too low, try to avoid bad feelings and even turn the situation around with some education.

First, put together a detailed price quote based on the project your client has in mind and the available budget. List the project's specifications and the estimated cost for each item. This will show the client exactly what it will cost to do the job according to the desired specifications.

Then prepare a list of the specifications their budget will buy. Walk your clients carefully through each list, so they can see how much more money it will take to complete the job the way they want it.

If your client still maintains that you must find a way to work within the unrealistic budget, suggest that your client call another designer for an estimate. Offer to provide a name or two. It won't take your client long to discover that he was the one out of line, not you. He just may be back with a new appreciation for you and more money to spend on the project.

Sometimes it's difficult to explain to clients that shaving costs on the printing will often cause the design itself to suffer and look second rate. To avoid "Client Shock Syndrome" when the final project is complete and delivered, bring samples of lesser quality printing jobs to the meeting when budget cuts are first being decided. The client can then see the results of opting for lower printing prices.

If the budget is tight but not unreasonable, there are many ways to stay within the budget without compromising the job's final quality. Ask your usual vendors and subcontractors if they can bend a bit on this project. They may be willing to take less with an occasional tight budget. (If the client will agree to put the vendor's or subcontractor's name on the finished piece, there's additional incentive for them to agree.) If not, try some other vendors and subcontractors. Check out companies that are just starting out in business; they will often give you a better rate than those who have

more than enough work.

If you can't reduce your fees without losing money, maybe you could find a freelancer whose fees are lower than yours to do all or part of the job. You can also reduce your markup on materials and outside services.

Finally, changing some of the project specifications can also bring the price down. Suggest that the client reduce the number of printed pieces, use fewer colors, or switch to a good but lesser quality paper. If you have a good working relationship with your printer, ask your contact there for other suggestions.

STAYING COMPETITIVE

You can only cut your costs so far to stay competitive. There will come a point when you simply cannot afford to reduce your prices any further. Know what your limits are and then abide by them.

When faced with a tough economy, you may be forced to cut your fees; cut your overhead or operating costs in direct proportion to your fee reduction, so you don't reduce your profits. Here are some alternatives you can explore:

• If you rent studio space, you can ask the landlord for a rent reduction for a specified period of time to ride out the market decline. Many landlords will do this during

tight times, rather than lose a good tenant.

• You can move into lower priced offices.

• You can operate out of your home.

• You can move in with another graphic artist or share space with a co-op group.

• You can cut back on salaries and benefits.

• You can reduce or eliminate staff and operate with part-timers or freelancers.

• You can cut office supply waste: recycle envelopes; use computer paper that's been printed on one side as scrap paper (if you can't run it through the printer again); or try to repair or refresh pens and markers. Look at the items you spend the most money on and see if you can find a way to stretch them further.

• You can reduce your business entertainment spending.

A good rule to follow is cut the small things so you can afford the big things. And when it comes to the big things, like relocating your office or cutting your staff, explore every option. Talk to your accountant to get some numbers on long-term planning. If you have employees, talk with them. They may have some great ideas, especially if it could mean their jobs.

Increase Marketing and Self-Promotion Efforts

The best alternative when you are faced with a business slowdown is to bring in new clients. I know that going after new business isn't fun, but now you have to do it.

The easiest way is to network with your printers, subcontractors, service bureau people, suppliers. Put the word out that you are ready to expand your client base; in fact, that is exactly the term to use. (Don't tell people that you desperately need new business.) You can also check out local business organizations such as the Chamber of Commerce, the Better Business Bureau and Women in Business.

Send out promotional flyers or other printed materials to potential clients, just to let people know you are around. Call clients who haven't done any work with you in a while, drop them a note, or put a promotional postcard in the mail. It's always amazed me how many times a client has said, "Thanks for the call, you reminded me that I do have this project I've been meaning to get to."

How you position yourself and your business in your particular market can make a big difference in attracting new clients. Make yourself stand out from those other designers who are trying to get the same clients you want.

Find out as much as possible about the specific clients you intend to target. You can then direct your efforts toward only those clients who want the specific skills, talents and services you have to offer. Call potential clients and ask what they want. Tell them you're doing a market survey and would like to know what's important to them when they hire a designer or illustrator. Also ask who they have hired in the past and what they expect their needs to be in the future. Don't ask for an interview during the call, but don't hesitate if someone asks about your work. You'd be surprised how many clients you can get this way.

GETTING PAID

You won't be in business long if you don't get paid on time or at all. It's not that most clients are disreputable and try to take advantage of you, but often they need to be reminded of an outstanding bill or an invoice that has fallen through the cracks of their bill-paying system. If you don't keep track of who owes you how much, you may never get paid.

Make it part of your weekly routine to check that you have billed for all work completed and part of your monthly routine to call those who haven't paid you. It's crucial to

keep your client billing moving at a steady pace, because clients can take a full thirty days from the time they receive a bill to pay it. The sooner you bill clients after a job is complete, the better your chances of using the clients' money to pay vendors, instead of dipping into your own business or personal savings.

When you begin working with a new client, be sure that your terms for payment are specified in the proposal or your working agreement. Establish a payment policy that stipulates the amount necessary to begin the project, and the payment schedule expected over the course of the project. If you want to have the project's balance paid in full upon delivery of the completed project, refuse to accept other terms. Regardless of how and when a client wants to pay you or is used to working, you can often set your own terms. If you run up against a client who will go elsewhere rather than agree to your payment terms, remember that your cash flow is more important than any client.

If you expect payment within thirty days and charge interest on all balances thereafter, state it. And then reinforce your policy by getting your bills out on time, including bills for delinquent payments, too.

When you have the client sign

the contract, ask how the company's bill-paying system works. Is the billing cycle thirty or fifteen days? These are better companies to work with than those who will pay at bimonthly or longer intervals. Find out when they issue checks so that you can arrange to send your invoice one week prior to their payment date. Otherwise, you will wait another thirty days. With companies on longer cycles, insist on payment on your terms, not theirs, and get that agreement in writing. If a client refuses, walk away. You don't need and can't afford to finance someone else's project.

When a Client Can't or Won't Pay

There are ways to get a client to pay without embarrassing him and preserve a good business relationship. Try to uncover the cause of the late payment. Sometimes a follow-up call will uncover dissatisfaction with the projects or the costs that need to be resolved. Other times a client will have temporary, minor cash flow problems, and you can work out a schedule of partial payments. However, take action quickly.

The sooner you go after someone who's late, the better your chances of collecting. Send a monthly statement that itemizes overdue balances. Add on interest at the rate of $1^1/_2$ percent for each remaining bal-

ance. The first time you send out a client statement with interest, stamp *Overdue* next to each balance that is beyond thirty days but under sixty. When a statement's balance has gone past sixty days, stamp it *Payment Due Upon Receipt*. Make follow-up calls after the client has had time to receive the notice.

Stamp any balances that go into the 120-day category *Payment Due Upon Receipt*, but also write in red pen next to the stamp, "Please contact us if there is a problem paying this bill upon receipt. Otherwise, if payment is not received within five business days, this matter will be turned over to an attorney." I always put a clause in my client contracts stating, "Client subject to reasonable attorney's fees if collection is necessary."

Send any notice indicating that collection action is imminent by certified mail, return receipt requested, so the client signs a receipt acknowledging delivery. That's your legal proof that you properly notified the client.

If you want to make a last ditch effort to resolve an unpaid bill, try writing a letter to the president of the company—if this person is not your contact. Explain clearly, but politely, your inability to collect payment. Attach copies of any items, such as contracts, production orders, price estimates and invoices, that support your position. Express your disappointment in the company and your regret that you will be forced to turn this over to an attorney. Then state that copies of this letter and all attachments are being sent to the Better Business Bureau, the state attorney general's office and local credit bureaus (list them by name). Also check with Dun & Bradstreet. If the company is listed with them, send copies. This may be all it takes to solve the problem. No business can run the risk of losing its credit rating and reputation.

When all your efforts to solicit payment from a client have failed, turn the matter over to a collection agency as a last resort. If you go the collection agency route, be prepared to lose a third of the balance due to the agency. They operate on a contingency basis, taking part of the balance if they collect. You may find it more effective and affordable to pursue bills of less than $1,000 in small claims court yourself rather than getting an attorney involved. While you may require a client to pay attorney's fees, there is no way to force payment.

I N D E X